The Elements of the Cosmos:
Numbers and Letters as Archetypes

by Scenza

With a Foreword by Christopher Gibson,
Past President of The Church of Light

Table of Contents

Acknowledgements

*This text would not have been possible, were it not for many
people, including but not limited to:
Christopher Gibson, Former President of The Church of
Light, who first invited and then helped to sustain the
creation of these articles;
Vicki Brewer, Margaret "Peg" Joscher, and the other members
of the Board of Directors of The Church of Light, for
supporting the compilation and realization of this text;
My wife, for her expert artistic rendering of the cover art and
formatting of this text;
My Mom, for instilling in me the greatest gift of faith,
without which such subjects might remain unexplored; and
The Lord, who inspires and motivates all things, including
this investigation.*

Foreword

The Hebrew Alphabet is familiar to every Jewish boy or girl who has attended Hebrew school in preparation for his or her Bar or Bat Mitzvah. Over the last two millennia, since the destruction of the Temple of Jerusalem in 70 CE, Jewish religion has been a religion of literacy. The focus is on scripture, the Torah or Jewish Bible and other scriptural materials. Every boy transitioning to manhood, becoming a full-fledged "son of the commandment", must prove his ability to read the Torah. Since 1922, this ritual has been made inclusive for girls on the threshold of becoming women and publicly acknowledged members of a community in reformed and reconstructionist Jewish sects.

Outside communities of Jewish coreligionists, the Hebrew Alphabet has long been the subject of scholarly and philosophical fascination. During the Italian Renaissance, scholars had access to books entering Europe due to the fall of the Byzantine Empire. An interest waxed for Classical Greek and Roman philosophers and poets, the Greco-Egyptian text of Hermes Trismegistus, and Jewish Kabalism, mathematics and algebra.

Humans have long been fascinated by numbers, both as an essential need for accountancy, but also as symbols of more abstract concepts and principles. There is evidence of prehistoric humans using notched bones and sticks as a means of numeric record keeping 40,000 - 45,000 years ago. By 4,000 BCE, more sophisticated accounting systems were evolving in ancient Persia, where clay tokens of different sizes could represent sheep or goats in units of one and ten. These tokens could be sealed into a clay envelope to be delivered to a recipient, essentially the first system of writing.

Nearby in Mesopotamia, the Sumerians also used clay to evolve their system of cuneiform writing 3,500 – 3,000 BCE. It was out of the need for accountancy that written communication was born. Almost simultaneously, in Egypt, from 3,400 – 3,200 BCE, hieroglyphs were first recorded, also using clay tablets. And one of the most widely used writing systems, the Phoenician alphabet, developed around 1,050 BCE, in the eastern Mediterranean, having evolved from an earlier Proto-Canaanite alphabet.

It was this 22-lettered Phoenician alphabet that diversified into numerous national alphabets, such as Aramaic and Samaritan, Anatolian and Greek. In the Near East, the Aramaic alphabet gave rise to Hebrew and Arabic scripts, while around the Mediterranean and beyond, the Greek Alphabet gave birth to various scripts, including Latin, Cyrillic, Runic, and Coptic.

In most of these early alphabets, including the Hebrew alphabet, letters doubled as numbers, allowing their use in mathematical calculation as well as the more esoteric use of numbers as symbols of more abstract philosophical and spiritual concepts. This marriage of numbers and letters evolved into Numerology, through which the numerical values of the letters in words, names, and concepts were used to investigate the mysteries of the Cosmos. The Pythagorean School was chief among the proponents of the spiritual significance of numbers and their corresponding geometric shapes.

The Hebrew alphabet lent itself to combining letters and numbers, and linking them to philosophical and spiritual symbolism. It is through this union that Kabalism, or mystical Judaism, was birthed. *The Elements of the Cosmos: Numbers and Letters as Archetypes* seeks to explore and elucidate the spiritual and philosophic symbolism of letters and numbers as found in the Hebrew alphabet.

From the Italian Renaissance through the Enlightenment, occult and esoteric authors sought to synthesize the relationship of letters, numbers, vibrations, and astrology to further contemplate the secrets of the universe.

By the late 19th Century, Eliphas Levi (Alphonse Louis Constant) had linked the Hebrew Alphabet to the Tarot, a marriage that continues to this day in certain Western Mystery School traditions. In *The Brotherhood of Light* tradition, the Hebrew letters are symbols or archetypes that have become linked to letters, numbers, astrological signatures, and Tarot Arcanum.

This volume of *The Elements of the Cosmos: Numbers and Letters as Archetypes* is the result of over six years of effort on behalf of the author who writes under the pseudonym, Scenza. While serving as editor of *The Church of Light Quarterly*, I was searching for contributing authors to submit to our publication. This tome was originally born of conversations I had with the author, who pitched his idea of an ongoing series of articles on a current passion of his, the hidden symbolism of the Hebrew Alphabet.

From the summer of 2013 through the summer of 2019, Scenza researched and wrote a new article every three months to be published in the following season's Quarterly. This book is the culmination of those efforts.

The writer offers a unique perspective on an ancient topic. In addition to evaluating the symbolism of the Hebrew letters from the traditional Kabalistic rubric of Idea, Number, and Form, he leads us into the contemporary study of Phonosemantics, which analyzes the connections between the sounds of the letters and their meanings as applied in language. The goal of these chapters is to stimulate the reader into thinking more profoundly about symbolism as a key for reflecting on the nature of the Cosmos.

I hope you enjoy contemplating this material as much as I enjoyed interacting with the author during the six years that this project evolved.

Christopher Gibson
Past President, *The Church of Light*
Albuquerque, New Mexico
May 2020

PREFACE

This book did not start out as a book at all. Rather, it began as a series of articles composed quarterly for *The Church of Light Quarterly* e-publication. Ten articles on the sacred numbers preceded twenty-two articles on the sacred letters of the Ancient Hebrew Alefbayt (AHA). A few additional introductory and conclusory articles rounded out the series. All told, the series took nearly ten years to complete, a fitting quantity in itself for such a project. As the collection of articles neared its natural conclusion, conversations began with Church of Light Officers about the possibility of amassing all of the articles into a single compilation for maximal efficiency and utility. This text is the result of those happy communications.

This book is divided into two main sections. The first set of approximately ten articles examines the sacred numbers through the lens of Sacred Geometry, proceeding from the Monad to the Decad. The arithmetic, geometric, and symbolic value of each number is discussed in turn. The second set of approximately twenty-two articles turns attention to the sacred letters of the Ancient Hebrew Alefbayt (AHA). Kabbalists claim that the AHA is a deliberately constructed alphabet, such that the sounds of the various letters are not random or haphazard, but rather that the sound of each letter is a deliberate sonic expression of its esoteric meaning. For example, the first letter of the AHA, Aleph, is not called so by accident, but rather because that sound best encapsulates its esoteric value. Aleph is defined by Kabbalists as a *guttural* consonant, produced deep in the throat, invisible to the viewer. As such, it is well representative of the concept of *spirit*- that which is also invisible to the eye, yet which animates and enlivens all other forms in the universe. Linguistically, Aleph is a sonic expression of the same archetype that is expressed conceptually as *spirit*.

To be sure, this is a bold assertion, and part of the premise of investigating the sacred letters of the AHA for these articles was to examine whether the author also affirmed such a relationship. While it is not yet possible to say with complete certainty that such a correlation exists between sound and symbolism in the AHA, a phenomenon termed *phonosemantics* in the linguistic literature, after having examined each of the twenty-two letters of the AHA in turn, *it is the assertion of the author that there are many compelling pieces of evidence in favor of such a conclusion.* Further studies are needed to either more completely bear out or else refute this tantalizing thesis.

Curiously, while the field of phonosemantics is very old and has been taken up by some of the greatest minds ever to people our planet, as its lively discussion in Plato's *Cratylus* convincingly attests, it is as yet heavily understudied and under-regarded. It is the hope of the author that this book will inspire and catalyze further investigation into this profound, thought-provoking topic.

Section I:

Numbers as Archetypes

INTRODUCTION

Quick: what is the sum of 1+2+3+4? A moment of cursory calculation will yield the obvious numerical sum: 10. However, what if I were to tell you that this simple, almost banal mathematical statement ensconces the basic creative principle of the entire Cosmos?

Over the course of ten articles, we will take a tour through the archetypal nature of number. We will look to understand how the arithmetic and geometric properties of each basic digit were studied by our ancient ancestors, in an effort to understand the unique universal symbolisms inculcated within them. We will then attempt to understand how ancient peoples encoded these truths into all aspects of their lives, including art, architecture, religion, science, and philosophy. Indeed, ours is no small undertaking, but any step towards understanding will help us to more deeply appreciate the awesome order with which God has imbued the "*Kosmos*", as it was known to Pythagoras. Let us begin our journey by seeking to explain the statement made at the beginning of this article, using it to take a brief tour through the ten basic numbers- the archetypes of the world.

Woefully, mathematics has been reduced in large part to a strictly practical exercise. Ask most people to answer the statement above, and they will arrive momentarily at a fixed, indisputable answer. However, numbers have not always been limited to such banal expressions. Certain groups of people- notably among them the Ancient Egyptian originators of groups such as The Church of Light- have perceived far deeper symbolisms in the ten digits which form the foundation of our counting system. By analyzing the arithmetic and geometric properties of these fundamental quantities, and by comparing them to their organic uses in nature, such thoughtful souls were able to sublimate simple whole numbers into deep, abiding, eternal truths.

How, then, can the above statement be symbolically interpreted, in order to reveal the basic process by which all things are created? That involves a brief explanation of the symbolic content of each number: the Monad (1), the Dyad (2), the Triad (3), the Tetrad (4), and their sum, the Decad(10). While superficially described here, each of these concepts will be much further developed in subsequent articles, along with the remaining digits from five to nine.

Imagine a point, dimensionless and timeless- existing in concept, but having no materiality. Suddenly, for reasons unknown, it expands outward endlessly, equally in all directions. It results in the most perfect of shapes: the circle. The circle has no beginning and no end; every point on its surface is equidistant from its center; and it is the most efficient shape, in that it encloses the most area within the smallest perimeter. This most inclusive of all shapes was taken by the Ancient Greeks to represent the Monad, or the principle of Oneness.

The Monad represents the beginning, without which there cannot be a middle or ending. It is the commencement of any particular enterprise; yet, without a sustained effort and conclusion, it amounts to little more than wishful thinking. It is utterly simple in its expression: in order to remain as the Monad, it must remain totally undifferentiated, uniform, and potential in its manifestation.

How, then, can the Monad, simplest of all shapes and principles, originate the incredible complexity of our universe?

For reasons unknown and by methods presently beyond understanding, this undifferentiated state of Oneness then contrareplicates itself, producing a quantity that is similar in design but opposite in polarity from itself. The second digit, the Dyad introduces the concept of opposites- inseparable pairs such as Black and White, Day and Night, or Wrong and Right. Tidily, each opposite points towards its counterpart, the one being incomplete without the other. However, in this primordial state, there is no connection or contact between these opposites. Existing in a state of constant tension and separation, these opposites are effectively polarized- as yet frozen in their inability to move forward in the process of creation.

That is, until a bridge is formed between them. Whether it is the subatomic force between the protons and electrons of atoms, the union of man and woman that produces a newborn baby, or the reciprocal forces of gravity which planets exert upon each other in order to maintain stable orbits, the interaction between opposites forms the basis for all activity in the universe. The mighty, eternal Triad has emerged, and with it, the beginnings of an intelligible universe which can be studied, described, and at least in some part, comprehended.

Yet, this triadic interaction of Monad and Dyad manages to do something truly miraculous along the way. As if this emergence of something from nothing were not incredible enough, the harmony of the Monad and Dyad to create the Triad achieves yet another miracle. *It lifts the original expression of the Monad to a new level of expression.* And in order to symbolize this shift, we must behold the Tetrad.

Using an example detailed previously, when protons and electrons are held together by subatomic forces, they almost magically create something altogether new: the atom. While all atoms are composed of the same basic subunits, i.e., protons and electrons (and neutrons in more complex atoms than Hydrogen), the various atoms which these subatomic particles comprise have properties that are entirely distinct from the subatomic particles themselves. For example, Hydrogen, the first and simplest element, is a highly explosive gas, while Helium, the next element in the Periodic Table of Elements, is extremely stable. This explains why the Hydrogen gas of early blimps was replaced by Helium: both are lighter than air, but Helium is far less likely to ignite and cause such horrific events such as The Hindenburg Explosion.

Numerically, the original trinity of Monad, Dyad, and Triad can be used to explain the basic processes by which anything is created. However, it is necessary to introduce the Tetrad, among other reasons, in order to signify that creation does end with the Triad, but rather that each ending is a new beginning, and merely heralds a new stage in the developmental process.

How fitting, then, that in our number system, the sum of the first four factors needed in order to describe the creation of the *Kosmos* itself and all within it enumerates the crowning principle of creation: the Decad? Symbolic of the original Monad brought to fruition and realization, it is the perfect sum of the processes of emergence, differentiation, harmony, and re-emergence. Indeed, $1 + 2 + 3 + 4 = 10$.

THE ETERNAL MONAD

The Ancient Greeks called the first quantity the Monad. According to Schneider (1994, p.2) in *The Beginner's Guide to Constructing the Universe*, the word monad derives from menien, meaning "to be stable", implying the Greeks' belief that the Monad well represented the first and eternal principle of all things. As such, it alternatively represented God, Spirit, Eternity, and all other concepts beyond space and time, which bore no beginning or end.

Recalling from the introductory article on this topic that the ancient mathematical philosophers understood numbers not only as quantities, but as geometrical figures, the seminal shape associated with the Monad is the circle. The circle is well representative of the principles of the Monad, in that it also is unchanging and stable, totally uniform all along its perimeter, and has no beginning or end. As such, it has been used since time immemorial as a symbol of the same principles as the Monad. For example, its use as a wedding band, to indicate the hope that a marriage should be deeply enduring, comes to mind.

Hence, when speaking of the Monad, it is equally effective to discuss the important symbolic aspects of a circle, as it represents spatially what the Monad represents quantitatively. Indeed, Brotherhood of Light members are already deeply familiar with this symbol, as it is the same as the astrological symbol for the Sun: ⊙. It is a *central point* set within a *space* marked out by a *perfectly uniform circle*. Let us discuss each of these critical parts of the symbol in turn.

The point at the center represents the concept of the Monad as a beginning. It is the seed from which all things come, and from which all enterprises are initiated. In this sense, then, it represents well that motivating Force of the Universe which in various cultures has been called God, YHWH, or Allah- among countless other titles. A true point is dimensionless, representing a state independent of space or time.

That point expands outward equally and uniformly in all directions to simultaneously create the boundary of the universe (represented in Western traditions by the Dyad) and the space which that boundary demarcates (represented in Western traditions by the Triad). The Circle, then, represents a great mystery: the Unity manifested as a Trinity. It can also be taken to express the journey from nothingness (represented by the point), to everything (represented by a circle with an infinite number of points on its surface), and all developmental stages in between.

The Monad also bears some very interesting arithmetic and geometric properties. As Schneider (1994) points out, $111111111 \times 111111111 = 12345678987654321$, indicating the all-encompassing role of the Monad arithmetically. Geometrically, the circle represents the single-most efficient two-dimensional shape in the universe. There is no other shape which encloses a greater area within a smaller perimeter. Hence, it also represents maximized efficiency.

This latter principle is borne out in several common examples. Ancient soldiers carried round shields because it allowed them the greatest protection for the least weight and material. Foodstuffs are sold most commonly in cylindrical cans because this shape allows the greatest amount of product to be contained in the smallest amount of space and material. The only more efficient three-dimensional shape is a sphere, but it could indeed prove difficult to stack spherical cans!

Hence, we discover in the Monad, and its corresponding geometric manifestation, the circle, an undying symbol of the eternal, the unchanging, and the perfectly equal. This, then, entitles it to represent, however imperfectly, that most effluent, unknowable, and incomprehensible Source of all: God. The Monad not only symbolizes the beginning of any process or endeavor, but also hints at its completion through its mysterious communication of a Trinity within a Unity. It describes a universe based on efficiency and balance. To Pythagoras and many of the other ancient mathematical philosophers, it epitomized the perfect shape. Detailing its hallmarks and characteristics, it is not at all difficult to see why.

The Dyad: Different and the Same

The Ancient Greeks called the second quantity the Dyad. The word *dyad* derives from "dia", meaning "through or asunder", implying the Greeks' belief that the Dyad was the first quantity to endure the agonizing process of separating from the perfect, whole Monad. As befits its polarity, the Dyad's separation is both a happy departure on the journey from one to many, but also a suffering step away from the perfection of the Monad.

How then did the ancient sacred geometers depict the movement of number from one to two, from unity to separation? As Schneider (1994) relates, they ingeniously conceived of the circle, symbol of the unity of the Monad, *as making a polar copy of itself*, quite alike in many details, but opposite in polarity. In this way, the *sameness* which is characteristic of the Monad produced *difference*, the hallmark of the Dyad.

Two circles offset from one another, each with its central point located anywhere on the circumference of the other (and thus still seen as deriving from it) create the seminal shape from which all other shapes will ultimately emerge: the *vesica piscis* (see illustration below). This almond shape has been captured and used in so many capacities that it is impossible to recount them all. They play into the shape of a cathedral's door, as well as the common and familiar "fish" of Christianity. In all cases, the *vesica piscis*, because of its basic association with the Dyad and polarity, hints at the process of parturition, or birth.

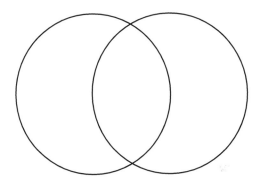

The vesica piscis, as the interface of two complementary opposites, symbolizes the birthplace of creation.

A second geometric figure which is closely associated with the Dyad is the line. The line again fits well the dual nature of the Dyad, in that it can act either as a barrier between two objects, or as a bridge between them. A true line is one dimensional in its nature, having length, but no depth or breadth. Curiously, as with the dimensionless point of the Monad, the truly one-dimensional line of the Dyad cannot be drawn in a three dimensional world, as it does not yet have width or depth. As detailed by Taylor (1816) in his seminal work, *Theoretic Arithmetic*, this hints at the fact that the first two quantities were not regarded by the ancient mathematical philosophers as numbers *per se*, but rather as *the parents* of number. As Schneider (1994) astutely points out, this generative role of the Monad and Dyad is further buttressed by the fact that *all shapes in the universe can be constructed by using a combination of the circle (i.e., Monad) and the line (i.e., Dyad)*. Once again, we are reminded of the Dyad's basic role in the creative process: it is through the re-union of polar opposites that new life is brought into being.

Extending a point to form a line moves the process of creation from its dimensionless beginning to a one-dimensional state of being.

Examples of this polar reunion abound in nature. Two oppositely charged particles, the proton and the electron, come together to form the most basic chemical element: Hydrogen. Two individuals of opposite biological sex unite to create a new human life. The polarization of opposites and their subsequent reunification (symbolized by the Triad) is at the heart of all creative processes.

The Dyad's position as a doorway or portal between the potential creative energy of the Monad and the actualized creation which will be represented by the Triad is also revealed in its uncanny arithmetic. The only quantity which, when added to itself is greater than its multiplicative product, is one. To state this mathematically: $1 + 1 > 1 \times 1$. The only number which, when added to itself is equal to its multiplicative product, is two. That is, $2 + 2 = 2 \times 2$. For all subsequent numbers, the product of the number multiplied by itself is always greater than the sum of the number added to itself. For example, $3 + 3 < 3 \times 3$; $4 + 4 < 4 \times 4$ …

This strange arithmetic behavior led the ancient mathematical philosophers to consider the Dyad as a sort of portal or gateway between the potential for creation symbolized by the Monad, and its actualization, as first achieved by the Triad. As it bridges these two disparate notions, it retains qualities of both. Two is both a barrier and a bridge. It represents a step forward in the evolution of numbers, but also a painful separation from the source. Fittingly, it is remarkably dual in nature. It cannot be defined simply as this *or* that, but is equally well described by this *and* that. It both distinguishes and rectifies two disparate things, in that an opposite cannot be fully understood without comparing it against its counterpart. For example, how can there be a complete knowledge of *day* without a consideration of *night*? Or how can the concept of *full* be completely comprehended without an equal contemplation of *empty*? In like manner, all opposites are both distinguished from and yet at least in part defined by their complements.

And so it is that the audacious, agonizing Dyad acts as both a moat and a drawbridge over the seemingly untraversable chasm between the Monad and the Triad. It is, at once, both different and the same.

THE TRIAD: MULTIPLICITY, COMPLETION, AND BALANCE

There is perhaps no more oft-quoted number in religious circles than three. Christians speak of The Father, Son, and Holy Spirit. Hindus talk of the Triune Godhead, composed of Brahma the Creator, Vishnu the Preserver, and Shiva the Destroyer. And, stemming from The Brotherhood of Light tradition, the three outer planets, which represent the forces precedent of the formation of the Universe, are Pluto, Neptune, and Uranus symbolizing respectively Life, Love, and Light. Why is the Triad held in such lofty esteem? For many reasons, no doubt, but chief among them is its use as a symbol of multiplicity, completion, and balance.

Recall that as detailed by Taylor (1816) in *Theoretic Arithmetic* and supported by Iamblicus (1988) in *The Theology of Arithmetic*, the Monad and the Dyad, were considered as *the parents* of numbers, but not as numbers themselves by the ancient mathematical philosophers. The Triad, then, is the first true number. For this reason, it was referred to as "the firstborn", or "the eldest" offspring of the mystical union between the Monad and Dyad. As the product of the union of the Monad and Dyad, it demonstrates aspects of both. Schneider (1994, p. 39) remarks that "it is the only number of infinitely many which is composed of the sum of all terms below it (3=2 +1)". No other number can be completely composed of all of its formative terms.

Also recall that the arithmetic of the Monad (1), Dyad (2), and Triad (3) differs in an essential way. The only quantity which, when added to itself is greater than its multiplicative product, is one. To state this mathematically: $1 + 1 > 1 \times 1$. The only number which, when added to itself is equal to its multiplicative product, is two. That is, $2 + 2 = 2 \times 2$. For all subsequent numbers,

12

the product of the number multiplied by itself is always greater than the sum of the number added to itself (e.g., 3 + 3 < 3 x 3; 4 + 4 < 4 x 4; ...). Hence, the Triad has been taken to represent "The Many".

Geometrically, whereas the Monad is represented by a dimensionless point, and the Dyad by a one-dimensional line, the linking of three distinct points in space permits the formation of the very first and simplest two-dimensional shape possible, the triangle. Even geometrically, we observe one lone point (representative of the Monad) in a system with a line (representative of the Dyad), coming together to create the first planar form, the triangle (i.e., the Triad).

The concept of Unity manifesting as a Trinity is central to theological thought. Even the word "trinity" itself connotes this concept: tri-unity. Indeed, a closer examination of the Monad, this time represented as a point within a perfectly symmetric and endless circle, reveals a trinity within a unity: the point, the radius, and the circumference. United in their purposes, these three aspects bring to *completion* the process of unfolding which began with the infinite potential of the Monad, and was issued forth through the Dyad.

But perhaps the most significant symbolism captured by the Triad is that of *balance*, for it is through the balance of antagonistic forces that life itself is generated and sustained. The positive proton and the negative electron interact in a delicate dance, permitting the creation of the very first physical element, Hydrogen. A man and a woman come together through the bond of love to procreate a human child. Even within the human body, this axiom holds true. *Anabolic* processes, or processes that build up larger molecules from smaller ones, are counterbalanced by *catabolic* processes, or processes that break down larger molecules into smaller ones. The balance of these two opposite forces is termed *metabolism*, and forms the basis of health. In all things, balance wins the day.

Perhaps the innate link between the Triad's principle of harmony and our own human make-up explains its fundamental importance in philosophies of all climes and times, with examples popping up from ancient through modern times, in countries as diverse as China, India, and Greece. Discussions of The Middle Way, The Golden Mean, and other balance-based perspectives all incline toward a point of virtue situated intermediately between two polar extremes of vice. By seeking balance and harmony in our own lives, we are renewing the eternal promise of the Triad: the One manifests as Many, and is sustained through the harmony of opposing influences.

THE TETRAD: BEGINNING AT THE END

At once, we come to both the end of a journey, and the beginning of another as we consider the symbolism of the Tetrad. Indeed, it would be very difficult to overemphasize the importance of the symbolism of the first four numbers to the mathematical philosophers of old, for in this simple, seemingly mundane sequence they ensconced some of their deepest spiritual wisdom.

The ancient seers left us a roadmap of their understanding of the universe in virtually every aspect of their society. Their worldview pervaded all of their fields of investigation, including but not limited to religion, architecture, art, music, and mathematics. Consistent themes emerge when any of these fields is studied in depth.

Their worldview begins from a perfect unity, termed in Number Theory the Monad. It is perfect, undifferentiated, and whole. However, it is completely simple and uniform-a far cry from the world of infinite diversity which we encounter on a daily basis. Hence, the Monad begins the process of differentiation by diverging into two distinct polarities, creating the world of opposites ruled by the Dyad. Now, contrary concepts such as day and night, right and left, emerge. However, these converse counterparts by their definitions must ever remain distinct, frozen in their seemingly untraversable distance from each other. It is only with the emergence of the Triad that a *relationship* between these polarities for the first time becomes possible. And with that interaction, symbolically all of the myriad combinations which lead to the diversity of our world erupt into being. Behold, the world is born!

It is glorious and joyous that the world of our experience and growth should be born, but how shall it be *reborn*? Shall it remain ever a stale, stagnant realm, wherein the same cycles endlessly repeat themselves? Or shall it constantly be in a state of not only creation, but *re-creation*: achieving goals, but then setting out new goals as soon as these former goals are achieved?

The latter is far more indicative of the world, and such symbolism is communicated through the Tetrad. The Tetrad symbolizes the completion of the process of creation which was depicted in the sequence from Monad to Triad. However, every ending in our universe is also a new beginning- a launching point for a new set of questions, a higher order of complexity. And so we must ask ourselves if it is accidental that our entire numerical system resolves down to this single, simple equation:

$$1 + 2 + 3 + 4 = 10$$

Symbolically, the Monad bridges the gap between simplicity and complexity through the Dyad, resulting in the multiplicity represented by the Triad. However, every completed system is also a starting point for a new system, as represented by the Tetrad. The sum of these four processes, the Decad, is a *new unity*, similar in many ways to the Monad, but expressing at a new level of complexity, having passed through a complete cycle of growth and development, as represented by the zero which follows the one in the construction of the number (i.e., 10).

This same concept has been communicated in myriad ways. For this is at least one interpretation of the famed Tetrakys of Pythagoras, as depicted below:

Here also there is an equivalence between The Tetrad and The Decad, as a great paradox is presented. As is explained in detail by Guthrie (1988) in *The Pythagorean Sourcebook and Library,* this diagram is both four and ten at the same time. It is four sequentially and ten cumulatively. An inextricable link is forever formed between these two numbers. They are both points of completion, as well as opportunities for new beginnings.

And is this not at least as aspect of the interpretation of the Holy Name, YHWH? In the Tetragrammaton, we discover a sequence of four letters so holy that it may not even be pronounced. Clearly, this sacred word must carry a message of great import. Perhaps part of its symbolism is that of the design and development of the universe itself, as portrayed arithmetically by the preceding mathematic formula, and graphically by Pythagoras' Tetrakys. In this Holy Name, we observe a deep-sighted effort to translate this same symbolism into the quintessence of sound itself.

The Tetrad completes the primary sequence of all number, a fundamental trinity which permits the movement from One to Many, as expressed and realized in its perfect result: the physical universe.

The Pentad: Life Emerges

As we arrive at the balance point in our journey through the numbers, we come to a new stage in the development of the universe. The first four numbers, taken from one perspective, can represent the four ancient elements of science: air, fire, water, and earth. To the ancient mind, they formed a blueprint for the design and creation of the universe. However, as is apparent to anyone who takes but a moment to observe, some physical entities are living while others are not. What then is the distinction between a living and a non-living entity?

The ancient sacred geometers discovered in the mathematics of the Pentad, the number Five, a symbol of the incredible burst of creative energy know as life. The development of an organism capable of evincing some degree of self-awareness must be a miracle of sorts within natural realms. While certainly we as human beings have much purification and improvement to undergo, still, the realization of organisms which can reflect upon and probe their environment and their own existence appears to be a unique and quite magical development in the history of the world. The ancient mathematical philosophers counted on the symbolism of the Pentad to communicate this momentous universal event.

Geometrically, the Pentad is closely linked with two shapes: the pentagon, a five-sided regular polygon, and the pentagram, a five-point star (see Figure 1).

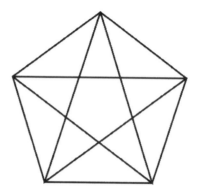

Figure 1: A pentagram inscribed within a pentagon.

Discreetly hidden within the unassuming shape of the pentagram, we find myriad examples of one of the simplest, yet most profound relationships in all of mathematics. The *Golden Section* abounds in the pentagram. The Golden Section is not a number, but rather a relationship between numbers. The diagram below (Figure 2) will help to explain this simple, yet substantial, ratio.

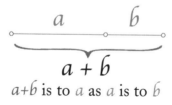

Figure 2: A line bisected according to the Golden Section.

In the diagram above, keep in mind that it is not the length of the line segments that is important, but rather *their relationships*. Line segment b is the shortest portion of the line. It bears a certain relationship to line segment a. According to the Golden

Section, line segment a must bear *the exact same relationship* to the whole line as line segment b bears to line segment a. To state this mathematically: *b/a = a/a + b*.

This relationship, discovered and revered since ancient times, is ubiquitous in nature. It has been used by architects in their design of cathedrals and religious edifices. It has been used in art to capture the natural proportions of living organisms. And it is part and parcel of the design of the human body. Consider for a moment that: the distance from the tip of the head to the chin, bisected by the brow, is a Golden Section; the distance from the elbow to the tips of the fingers, bisected by the wrist, is a Golden Section; the distance from the top of the head to the feet, bisected by the navel, is a Golden Section. Numerous additional examples exist, and have been used by the world's artistic masters to capture the "ideal" form of the human body. Indeed, it may very well be fair to state that what we think of as "beauty" is a tacit expression of this singular mathematical constant, known contemporarily as φ, the Greek letter *phi*.

The special and unique quality of φ is that it is a self-replicating line. It copies itself in such a way that the relationship of the shorter line to the longer line is exactly the same as the relationship of the longer line to the total line. This relationship can also be extended infinitely in either direction. That is to say, a line *of any length* may be divided according to the Golden Section, and that line will always bear the exact same numerical relationship: φ. The sacred geometers of old saw in φ a symbol of life itself, for one of the key criteria in determining whether something is living or non-living is whether or not it can reproduce more of its own kind. Living things of all types must achieve this, and φ, through its simple profundity, achieves exactly this.

As Schneider (1994) well explains, the pentagram, a regular

five-pointed star, is also replete with this constant. Additionally, a special quality of the pentagram is that it can be extended infinitely in either direction (see Figure 3). Its hallmark is *regeneration and replication*, just as one of the essential qualities of a living organism is its capacity to reproduce more of its own kind.

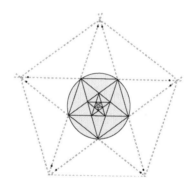

Figure 3: Pentagrams can be inscribed within pentagrams endlessly.

Hence, owing to its unique mathematical properties, the Pentad has come to be synonymous with that unique and special gift of the Creator, the beginning and end of all things: Life.

The Hexad: Balance Perfected

In my investigations, coming to a clear, one-word summary of the esoteric symbolism of the number 6, the Hexad, has been more problematic than for the previous integers. While there is a fair amount of commentary on its nature, no absolutely clear, single-pointed thread of meaning has emerged from my research. Hence, I have pored even more carefully and thoughtfully over these sources, and present here an inspiration which I hope will serve the symbolism of this number well.

One of the dominant symbolisms communicated by the Hexad is the principle of *symmetry*. In this sense, I mean a perfect, equilibrated state in which all subordinate forces are working in absolute harmony with each other. While the Triad, a close relative of the Hexad as equal to exactly half of its quantity, communicates the idea of harmony, the Hexad develops this concept further in order to indicate the symmetry of all parts and pieces of the system in question.

First of all, notice that the number itself occurs very close to the mid-point between 1 and 10. This in itself hints at the concept of its symmetric nature. Then, consider that the six-pointed star, which is ubiquitous with the Jewish faith, and forms a conspicuous aspect of The Brotherhood of Light logo as well, is itself an intimation of two opposing forces in absolute symmetry. One trine faces upward, while the other points down, balancing each other perfectly. Next, consider the unique arithmetic properties of the Hexad, as detailed by Iamblicus (1988), Nicomachus of Gerasa (2015), Schneider (1994), and Taylor (1816). To be sure, there are many, but one of the most unique arithmetic properties is that six is *the first perfect number*, in that:

$1 + 2 + 3 = 6$, and $1 \times 2 \times 3 = 6$. This is indeed a very rare phenomenon in mathematics, and demonstrates yet another form of symmetry and balance displayed by the Hexad. However, in order to even more deeply appreciate the myriad indications that the Hexad relates to a state of symmetry and equilibrium, we much delve even deeper.

Why is it that honeybees, for example, compose their hives of hexagonal compartments? Interestingly, as Schneider (1994) relates, this configuration minimizes labor and material, while maximizing space and strength. He goes on to explain that "due to the space-filling strength of the hexagonal shape …, the least wax is used to hold the most honey" (Schneider, 1994, p. 196). Hence, hexagonal geometry offers an ideal balance between structure and function.

As a teacher of Human Anatomy & Physiology, I am constantly stressing the importance of the inseverable link between these two concepts to my students. In the human body, as elsewhere, the structure, or anatomy, of an organ is inextricably tied in to its function, or physiology. Consider, for example, the heart. Its primary function is to pump blood throughout the body. Its shape, therefore, is well suited to this function. It is a hollow-bodied, rugged, muscular organ. Indeed, it is a basic tenet of Human Anatomy & Physiology that structure and function are inseparably interdependent, and that one can therefore follow the thread of one in order to begin to draw conclusions about the other.

The Hexad epitomizes the symmetry that maximizes the careful, delicate balance between form and function. Consider an additional example from Biology. According to The Cell Theory, the cell is the basic unit of life. Additionally, all living things must be composed of cells. Living things can be further categorized as either unicellular, such as a bacterium, or multicellular, such as a human being. A question arises in science as to why macroscopic life forms become multicellular, as opposed to simply existing as one very large cell. It turns out that there is a very reasonable response to this question.

The main argument given for why cells are limited in size has to do with the relationship between two different geometric concepts. The total area of the surface of a cell is termed its **surface area**. The inner contents of the cell, in other words the amount of space it takes up, comprises its **volume**. Surface area is flat, and therefore essentially a two-dimensional measurement, while volume describes the amount of three-dimensional space that an object takes up.

Cell are three-dimensional, and therefore contain volume. However, cells interact with their environment through an essentially two-dimensional barrier known as the cell membrane. It is through this barrier that the cell obtains its nutrition and removes its waste. *Therefore, a cell can only increase its volume to the point where it can continue to get enough nutrients in and wastes out through the surface area of its cell membrane.*

We can use mathematics to arive at some even more precise results. In order to simplify our calculations, it is reasonable to consider a cell to be roughly cubical (as many plant cells are). When this is the case, we can use the simple formula *6(side²)* in order to calculate any surface area (Recall that the faces of a cube are squares, and that there are six of them). The volume of a cube is also relatively easy to calculate as *length x width x height*, or in the case of a cube, *side³*.

If we consider a cube of side=1, then the surface area is 6 units (1x1x6), and the volume is 1 unit (1x1x1). The ratio of surface area to volume can therefore be summarized as 6:1. In this case, there is ample surface area to support the internal volume of the cell. If we consider instead a cube of side=2, then the surface area is 24 units (2x2x6), while the volume is 8 units (2x2x2). This means the ratio of surface area to volume is now 24:8, or more simply, 3:1. *Notice that the amount of surface area available in order to nourish the cell has just been cut in half!* It follows logically that the bigger a cell gets, the less relative surface area it will have to support its interior volume.

Very interestingly, a critical threshold is reached where the cellular surface area and the cellular volume are completely in balance, after which a cell must divide, because, growing larger than this critical threshold puts the cell at a disadvantage, as it no longer has adequate surface area to support its volume. *As you may have mused by now, the perfect balance point between surface area and volume occurs when the cube is considered to have a side 6 units long!* Consider the simple math: SA= 6x6x6=216; V=6x6x6=216. This makes the ratio of surface area to volume exactly 1:1, demonstrating with perfect mathematical precision that a cell can grow no larger and still maintain the ideal ratio between surface area and volume. While it is an example from the musings of a scientist, it is very curious at the least that this phenomenon occurs *only* with a cube with sides of exactly 6 units in length.

Summarizing, we observe in the Hexad the perfection of form that we term symmetry. It achieves the perfectly poised balance of structure and function, form and performance. It bears within itself the hallmarks of harmony introduced by the Triad, but brought to a more perfect and complete expression in the Hexad.

The Heptad: Divine Virgin

We arrive next in our analysis of the ten archetypal quantities to the number seven, the Heptad. Even a casual glance at various world religions and myths reveals copious references to the sacred Heptad. Seven is perennially perceived as a holy, pure number, and is always referenced on the side of truth and right.

There are several reasons for the association of the Heptad with these ideals. An important consideration deals with two very simple mathematic equations: $3 + 4 = 7$; and $3 \times 4 = 12$. This close relationship between 7 and 12, as both being comprised according to different mathematical operations of 3 and 4, is crucial to an understanding of the Heptad's symbolism.

As detailed by Nicomachus of Gerasa (2015) and Taylor (1816), odd numbers, in that they cannot be divided into equal parts, are considered as partaking of the nature of the Monad, and therefore are typically associated with the principle of spirit. Even numbers, as being divisible into two equal parts, are more closely associated with the Dyad, and therefore the principle of spirit's polar opposite, matter. Additionally, recall that the Monad and Dyad were not considered as numbers in and of themselves by the ancient mathematic philosophers, but rather as the parents of number. Hence, the Triad, as the first truly odd number, is representative of the inner, spiritual essence, while the Tetrad, as the first truly even number, is often associated with physicality and matter. *The Heptad, then, being composed of the sum of the Triad and the Tetrad, represents the perfect, balanced expression of spirit and matter.* The symbolism of the Dodecad (i.e., 12), as being composed of the product of the Triad and Tetrad is similar in its symbolism to that of the Heptad. However, in a further expression of their respective oddness and evenness, the Heptad, being odd, is taken to represent the hidden, esoteric side of creation, while the Dodecad, being even, symbolizes the manifest, exoteric perfection of creation. Another way of expressing this is to say that the Heptad represents the non-physical *process* of generation, while the Dodecad represents the physical *result* of that process.

As Schneider (1994) relates, of all the numbers in the Decad, the one which is said to be most similar to the perfect Monad, symbol of God and the source of all things, is the Heptad. Like the Monad, it was called "virgin", in the sense that no other number within the Decad enters into it evenly (e.g., as 2 enters 4, or 3 enters 6). It is also called "childless", in that the Heptad cannot produce any other number within the Decad through multiplication (as 2 produces 4, or 3 produces 6 and 9). Also, interestingly, of all the quantities between 1 and 9, *the Heptad is the only number which cannot divide 360, the number of degrees in a circle, evenly.* Hence, in truth, it is never possible to draw a perfect heptagon. The ancients took this as an eternal reminder of the presence of the innumerable, innominable, indescribable spirit which animates matter- omnipresent, eternal, elusive, and yet in many senses, more real that the transient, mutable, world it enlivens.

Music, colors, astrology, tarot, alphabets, and myriad other fundamental precepts all involve the Heptad in their explication of natural phenomena. Seven notes of the musical scale move our souls, and then repeat at a higher octave. Seven prismatic colors combine to produce white light. The movements of seven inner planets are analyzed more carefully in personal Astrology, as the outer planets move so slowly, that they are largely taken into account generationally. All of these systems and many more reveal a seven-fold process by which things move into and out of being.

For all of these reasons and more, the Heptad was held in the highest esteem by the ancient mathematical philosophers. Eternal, elusive, occult, it represents the pure and perfect fusion of our spiritual and material selves. It reminds us of a greater Reality which gives rise and reason to the cosmos.

The Octad: Same Difference

Leaving the pristine, ethereal realm of the Heptad, we re-enter the material world through the gateway of the Octad. As detailed by Nicomachus of Gerasa (2015) and Taylor (1816), excepting the Monad, which provides the blueprint for all number, the Octad is the only number within the Decad that is the product of a cubic calculation (2 x 2 x 2 = 8), indicating its link with three-dimensionality and the physical world. Again, in stark contrast to the "virgin" properties of the Heptad discussed earlier, the Octad is instead "promiscuous", in the words of Michael Schneider, author of *A Beginner's Guide to Constructing the Universe* (1994, p. 268), in that it is divisible by more terms than any other whole number within the Decad (i.e., 4, 2, and 1). Nicomachus of Gerasa (2015) and Taylor (1816) explain that the ancients called it "evenly even", in that all of its divisors are even, all the way down to the Monad. This is in contrast, for example, to the Hexad, which is considered "oddly even", because its divisors are **3,** 2, and 1.

The Octad occupies a unique position within the Decad, in that it demonstrates two symbolisms concurrently. The main theme of the Octad is *periodic renewal*. For this reason, depending on one's perspective, it can be seen either as the culmination of one process, or the beginning of a new round of development. Hence, Western musical scales are based on seven tones, but it is only with the return to the eighth, or octave, that they demonstrate completion and recommencement. Likewise, several elements in the Periodic Table of Elements demonstrate periodicity, becoming most stable when their outer energy levels house exactly eight electrons. We ourselves have fashioned our calendars on a similar principle, the standard week being comprised of seven days, and returning to the first day of a new week on the eighth day of the series.

Even the shape of the number itself (**8**), if studied carefully, reveals its symbolism. It is essentially two circles touching at a mid-point. A circle is an obvious symbol of a cycle. Hence, in the Octad, we see evidence of two cycles- one just finishing, the other just beginning. By depicting the same symbol horizontally instead of vertically, we arrive at the modern glyph for infinity (∞), a constant and eternal movement between the polar boundaries of any form of manifestation.

The paradoxical quip "same difference" is well-suited to describe the Octad. Consider a person completing a high school degree: in one sense, that individual is considered to have mastered certain material in order to be awarded that degree. And yet, once the party is thrown, she finds herself a beginner all over again upon entering the halls of a university. Our heroine is, at once, accomplished and a novice.

The Octad works in much the same way, in that it depicts the movement from one level of complexity to the next, or from one order of achievement to the following. It demonstrates sameness, in that it is a renewal of the original theme come back upon itself. Yet that renewal is distinctly different, in that it has now attained to a higher level of organization. Like a couple having a baby, that child is at once a part of them, yet at the same time a completely novel, unique individual. The child bears infinite possibilities, capable of anything in such a pure, nascent state. Likewise, we can see the Octad functioning in our lives wherever there is a repeated cycle, a folding back of one end upon a new beginning. And just as with a new baby, the possibilities for us, too, are endless.

THE ENNEAD: LIMIT & COMPLETION

The number 9, the Ennead, is the greatest of the single digits. As such, it represented in the minds of the ancient mathematical philosophers the limit of all processes, the culmination of all events. Embodying these principles, Schneider (1994) shares with us that they derived such epithets for it as "limit" and "horizon". Iamblichus (1988) adds that as a triad of triads (3 + 3 + 3 = 9), they labeled it "thrice perfect" and "thrice sacred", referencing the mystical qualities of the Triad, expressed in its totality on the spiritual, physical, and mental planes of being.

Mathematically, the Ennead displays a very interesting behavior indeed. As C.C. Zain (1994, p. 139) points out in *Course 6: Sacred Tarot*, the Ennead "possesses the unique property that it may be multiplied by any number and the digits so obtained when added together always resolve into 9." Zain likens this mathematical behavior to an expression of Manifest Deity, in that no matter what number we start from we always arrive at 9, and no matter what illusory form Deity may take in manifestation, that form always resolves down to one pure, perfect, unchanging Source.

The Ennead is also the only number in the Decad which is the sum of two cubes (1x1x1=1; 2x2x2=8; 1+8=9). As the cube is well associated with the Tetrad and solidity, completion and form, this only bolsters the Ennead's reputation as depicting a state of wholeness. And in countless examples, when a complete manifest unit is being depicted, we see a unified whole represented as 9 discrete archetypes. The Ancient Egyptian *neteru*, or pantheon of 9 supreme gods is an example, as are the Greek muses, designed to represent the full potential and expression of the arts and sciences. Indeed, even in our fast-paced, decidedly secular culture, we still see a panel of exactly 9 Supreme Court Justices, who preside over law in the United States, and act as the supreme authority over what is legal or illegal in our nation.

But perhaps the best example of the Ennead as a symbol of completion, perfection, and readiness to cross over into a new domain of expression occurs in the gestation and birth of a new human organism. Under ideal conditions, it takes exactly nine months for a new human organism to fully form. During this time, one of the absolute miracles of the universe unfolds, as a series of physical and chemical changes occur, more or less unbidden and unprompted by the mother, which ultimately result in the birth of a new human organism with untold potentials. Indeed, while admittedly I am musing at this point, it would not surprise me one iota if the very reason that we count with a decimal system based on 9 discrete digits which cycle infinitely towards either greatness or smallness, is because the Ancients saw in the organization and birth of a new human being an example of the very essence and purpose of existence.

Life is, has been, and always will be the greatest miracle. Indeed, members of the Brotherhood of Light reaffirm this every time they greet each other, saying *"Life, Love, and Light"*. Notice that it is Life which is uttered first, for it is the *sine qua non* upon which all else is based. If it were not for Life, or existence itself, nothing else could ever be present. There would be no experience whatsoever, and God would be all alone, infinite in potential, but without a single thing to show for it. Hence, I hope you will not think it too bold of me to declare Life the original and everlasting miracle, for through it all organisms are able to quest onward towards greater affection, or Love, and greater knowledge, or Light.

THE DECAD: AND THE LAST SHALL BE FIRST

The Decad is the masterful culmination and realization of the creative process which began with the Monad, and stepwise worked its way through all of the archetypes represented by the single digits. Its mathematical symbol, 10, depicts its nature perfectly: it is both the completion of one cycle, as indicated by the 0, as well as the initiation of a new round of evolution and growth, as represented by the 1. Juxtaposing these two numbers expresses quantitatively the timeless process of creation by which all things are manifested.

Indeed, as was discussed in the very first article of this series, the basic mathematical equation $1 + 2 + 3 + 4 = 10$ may reveal much about the ancient mathematical philosophers' cosmogony. Obviously, this statement is a mathematical equality, but if we treat it similarly to the manner in which we have been treating the numbers – that is to say, not only as quantities, but as possessing *qualities* – then, metaphorically this statement says that it takes no less than four discrete steps and ten independent archetypes in order to effect a complete cycle of creation. If we step back from our modern world, and consider the knowledge which it would take an ancient culture to derive such a statement, it is nothing short of awe-inspiring. This statement reveals an understanding of the three-dimensional nature of creation in our universe, and the fact that even the simplest three-dimensional figure, the tetrahedron, requires no less than four distinct evolutions in order to manifest. It is possible that the ancient mathematical philosophers extended this basic premise, thereby developing a philosophy and understanding of the cosmos from it.

Originally, the world is dark and void. It exists, yet it has no shape or form. It is in the state of the undifferentiated Monad-existing, but having no distinction or difference. Then, a magical event occurs: the Monad diverges into two discrete, polarized quantities, thereby revealing the Dyad. Yet, in this immature state, where only opposites exist, there is no communication, no bridge between these entirely disparate entities. With the advent of the Triad, for the first time there is an opportunity for *relationship*. This capacity for communication is first revealed in the trinity of the Monad, Dyad, and Triad.

Yet, life is infinite in its potential. It is myriad in its manifestations. How, then, could life remain simply three-fold, existing and communicating, yet unable to evolve any further? The emergence of the Tetrad completes the picture. The Tetrad, in a vein very similar to the Decad, is at once a completion and a new point of origin. It is on one hand the realization of the creative process initiated by the Monad, and on the other hand, offers the fresh hope of an ever expanding, ever diversifying world. There are countless examples of this in the universe, but the one thing they all share in common is the mystifying fact that a united Triad, as manifest in the Tetrad, takes on a whole new order of complexity and capacity. It is at once equal to the sum of its parts, but at the same time, something greater. Consider the following examples: protons, electrons, and neutrons come together in discrete quantities, yet somehow when they are united, they advance to a new level of complexity, the chemical element. This element, though composed of a quantifiable number of subatomic particles, somehow takes on properties that none of the particles independently bear.

Or consider a more familiar example: a man couples with a woman, and they bear a child. They are three separate, discrete, unique individuals. And yet, when they come together, they create a new level of complexity- the family. This family, as with the atom, is identifiably composed of certain individuals. And yet, the nuances of communication and potential which occur when they are united seem to outpace any basic quantification of their independent abilities.

It is perhaps a fundamental miracle of the world that this jump in complexity occurs when a certain number of factors come together. It is the basis of all of the rich and awesome diversity which fills our world, and whatever countless others might exist. And all of this is revealed, metaphorically, in the simple sum 1 + 2 + 3 + 4 = 10.

Section II:

Letters as Archetypes

THE SACRED HEBREW ALPHABET: INTRODUCTION-PART I

Much has been written about the sacred nature and structure of the Hebrew Alphabet. In fact, Kabbalistic literature boldly asserts that God created the Universe itself with the Hebrew letters (Munk, 1983, p.19). Considered from at least one perspective, however, this can very well be explained and understood. The twenty-two letters of the Hebrew Alphabet, more properly known as the Alefbayt (AB), stand in as archetypes in the design of Creation. For example, Aleph, as the first letter of the Hebrew Alphabet symbolizes, among other things, the principle of Unity and Oneness. Certainly, there is a place for the study and purpose of Oneness somewhere in God's Creation. And so it is for the other 21 letters that follow- each one, in addition to its linguistic function, symbolizes an archetypal form. Perceived in this light, we are far more justified in claiming that God created the Universe with the letters of the Alefbayt.

According to Kaplan (1997), there are three traditional levels of interpretation which Kabbalists apply to the Hebrew letters: idea, number, and form. The idea behind the letter is expressed by its name, as well as other Hebrew words which are very closely related to that name. The number, or gematria, is used to draw further inferences about the letter. Through the summation of the numeric equivalents of the letters that make up Hebrew words, links are often drawn between words which have the same numeric value, adding an additional level of homiletic interpretation. Finally, the manner in which the letter has been written (i.e., its form) has been painstakingly analyzed and further used to try to distill knowledge and understanding about the letter. In this series of articles, while relying closely on these three traditional levels of interpretation, a fourth level of potential meaning will be analyzed: that of the actual sound of the letter.

Each letter of the Alefbayt is associated with a specific sound, much as is the case in English. However, unlike English, Kabbalists claim that in Ancient Hebrew (AH), the relationship between the sound of the letter and the idea, number, and form of the letter are not haphazard, but rather form an intentional harmony which further expresses the occult value of the letter. Over the course of the several years which it will take to compose these articles, the author will endeavor to determine if any evidence of a connection between sound and meaning exists in Biblical Hebrew (BH).

The field of Linguistics recognizes the possibility of a link between sound and meaning, though mainstream Linguistics accepts the Saussurian ideal that "the sign is arbitrary" (Magnus, 2001, p. 24). In this case, the sign refers to a word, and it means to express the generally accepted notion that in the formation of languages, the particular word that a group of people decide to use to represent a thing or idea does not contain any deeper sound symbolism, but is rather simply agreed upon by that populace, and therefore comes to bear that meaning. For example, while English speakers use the word "dog" to describe a furry animal which is man's best friend, Spanish speakers call the same organism "el perro", and Italian speakers would refer to the same organism as "il cane". As disparate speakers in different parts of the world use different words, or signs, to refer to the exact same animal, one cannot help but conclude that the assignment of a particular word to an animal, or any object or idea, is at least in part arbitrary.

However, while there certainly appears to be some level of arbitrariness in the formation of words, several researchers, such as Bollinger (1950), Magnus (2001), Kirtchuk (2011), and even Plato (n.d.) have argued convincingly that there is a link between sound and meaning in certain cases. The formal study of this link is called phonosemantics, and it is a thoroughly thought-provoking branch of Linguistics.

Many Kabbalists claim that such an association exists between the letters of BH and their sounds. Accordingly, over the course of the next several years, the author will seek to investigate whether such a claim appears true or false. In order to do so, I will be relying heavily on authoritative Kabbalistic texts, such as the *Sefer Yetzirah* (Kaplan, 1997) and *The Wisdom in the Hebrew Alphabet* (Munk, 1983). However, in addition to these Kabbalistic works, I will also undertake my own investigations into the values and meanings of Hebrew words, and study them directly to discern if any link between sound and meaning is apparent. I am excited to embark on this journey into the ancient Alefbayt, and I welcome you to voyage with me into these new, uncharted, invigorating waters!

THE SACRED HEBREW ALPHABET: INTRODUCTION-PART II

While it would be wonderful to jump right into an analysis of the letters of the Ancient Hebrew Alphabet (AHA)- their allegorical, numeric, formal, and even phonetic meanings- careful analysis reveals that one more introductory article, in order to establish certain key parameters of the investigation, is warranted. The table on the following page summarizes key information, primarily derived from Aryeh Kaplan's (1997) *Sefer Yetzirah (p. 22, 178, & 198)*, a text well established as authoritative and insightful within the Kabbalistic tradition, with additional insights provided by the author.

Letter	Name	Meaning	Number (Serial/Gematria/Serially within a set of three clusters-Mother/Double/Single letter)	Designation	Phonetic Family (Traditional)	Astrological Correspondence (Short Version, Raavad)
א	Aleph	Ox	1/1/1-1	Mother	Guttural	Pluto
מ/ם	Maym/Final Maym	Water	13/40/1-2	Mother	Labial	Neptune
ש	Shin	Tooth	21/300/1-3	Mother	Dental	Uranus
ב	Bayt	House	2/2/2-1	Double	Labial	Saturn
ג	Gimel	Camel	3/3/2-2	Double	Palatal	Jupiter
ד	Dalet	Door	4/4/2-3	Double	Lingual	Mars
כ/ך	Kaph/Final Kaph	The hand bent	11/20/2-4	Double	Palatal	Sun
פ/ף	Pay/Final Pay	Mouth	17/80/2-5	Double	Labial	Venus
ר	Raysh	Head	20/200/2-6	Double	Dental	Mercury
ת	Taw	Cross	22/400/2-7	Double	Lingual	Moon
ה	He	Window	5/5/3-1	Single	Guttural	Aries
ו	Waw	Hook	6/6/3-2	Single	Labial	Taurus
ז	Zayin	Weapon	7/7/3-3	Single	Dental	Gemini
ח	Chayt	Fence	8/8/3-4	Single	Guttural	Cancer
ט	Tayt	Snake	9/9/3-5	Single	Lingual	Leo
י	Yod	Hand	10/10/3-6	Single	Palatal	Virgo
ל	Lamed	Ox-goad	12/30/3-7	Single	Lingual	Libra
נ/ן	Nun/Final Nun	Fish	14/50/3-8	Single	Lingual	Scorpio
ס	Samech	Prop	15/60/3-9	Single	Dental	Sagittarius
ע	Ayin	Eye	16/70/3-10	Single	Guttural	Capricorn
צ/ץ	Tzade/Final Tzade	Fish-hook	18/90/3-11	Single	Dental	Aquarius
ק	Quph	Back of the head	19/100/3-12	Single	Palatal	Pisces

In the first column, the form of the Hebrew letter is presented. As previously explained, many Kabbalistic sages have attempted to peer into the physical shape of the letter, and have yielded thoughtful, meaningful insights, which will be shared as appropriate over the course of these articles.

The second column provides an English pronunciation for each of the names of the letters. As we are moving from one alphabet to another, these are approximations, and have been rendered slightly differently by different authors. However, these names are very close to the original pronunciations.

The third column provides the meaning of the Hebrew name of the letter. As Biblical Hebrew (BH) is a consonantal language, several different words may all be spelled the same consonantally. Hence, while the meaning stated is considered the dominant meaning, it is also instructive to consider *all* of the Hebrew words that are consonantally spelled the same as the Hebrew name of the letter. To explain further, in traditional Biblical Hebrew no vowels are used. These would have been known by native speakers, and passed down from generation to generation. As in English, then, figuring out which of a small cluster of meanings should be applied to a particular word was a matter of context. As an English example, consider the following: "Th dg brkd." In this case, no vowels are used, but most well-versed English speakers would discern that the sentence probably indicates, "The dog barked." In similar fashion, well-versed speakers of Biblical Hebrew would have been able to apply the proper vowels, and therefore determine the exact meaning of the word via context.

The fourth column considers the numerical values of the letters. Three distinct numerical values are related, each communicating valuable information about the letter. The first term states the letter's serial placement within the Alefbayt. The second term relates the traditional gematria of the letter. Lastly, the third set of numbers represents the letter's placement within one of three clusters. The AHA has three different types of letters: Mother Letters (Group 1), Double Letters (Group 2), and Single Letters

(Group 3). The three Mother Letters, Aleph, Maym, and Shin, are associated with the three outer planets Pluto, Neptune, and Uranus, respectively. The seven Double Letters are associated with the seven inner planets, listed in order of their *period of revolution*, from longest to shortest. Finally, Group 3 is composed of the 12 Single Letters, which are traditionally associated with the 12 signs of the Zodiac, in their chronological order.

To offer a discrete example, let us consider Column 4 as relates to the letter, Maym. The column lists the following information: 13/40/1-2. The first number, 13, is the serial value of Maym, which is to say that it is the thirteenth letter of the AB. The second term, 40, is the traditional gematria of Maym. Finally, the third set of numbers, 1-2, states that Maym is in Group 1 (i.e., Mother Letters), being the second term within that series. All of these various ways of examining the numerical values of the AHA letters yield insights into their symbolisms.

The fifth column indicates the designation of each letter as belonging to one of three distinct clusters: the mother letters, the double letters, and the single letters. While well known within Kabbalistic circles, these designations take on special importance in this work, as they were in part used to determine the astrological correspondences of the letters. For example, as there are exactly three mother letters, and as there are exactly three outer planets, the assumption has been made that there is a correspondence between these two triads. While any assumption bears risk, this seems reasonable, as the seven double letters are traditionally associated with the seven inner planets, and the 12 Single Letters are traditionally associated with the twelve signs. By process of elimination, it appears quite reasonable that the three Mother Letters would be associated with the three outer planets.

A final word might be added here that the exact order of

association between the letters and astrological phenomena is an issue of debate even within Kabbalistic circles. How much more so, then, will variation exist from tradition to tradition? The astrological correspondences provided here are different than those within the Brotherhood of Light tradition. This, however, is not as large an issue as it might appear. As just mentioned, even *within* the Kabbalistic tradition, different sages derive different correspondences between the letters and celestial phenomena. The system which will be elaborated in these articles is well attested within Kabbalistic literature, and in the opinion of the author, is a clear, cogent, neatly logical association. Essentially, the three mother letters are associated serially with the three outer planets based on their *periods of revolution*, while the seven double letters are associated serially with the seven inner planets (also ordered based on their periodicity), and the twelve single letters are associated chronologically with the twelve zodiacal signs.

The sixth column bears special importance in this particular set of articles, as it sets out the traditional assignment of the letters into five linguistic classes. Recall that Biblical Hebrew is an ancient language, and as such, its language classifications will likely differ markedly from those of modern Linguistics. In this work, the author has employed the original BH classifications, in the hopes that the original intentions of the architects of the Hebrew language will have a greater likelihood of shining through. Where appropriate and for context, the modern linguistic classifications of these letters will also be provided.

According to Kaplan (1997), the five linguistic categories into which the twenty-two AHA letters are organized are based on their points of articulation in the vocal tract. When most speech sounds are uttered, a stream of air is emitted from the lungs. In some cases, the air is then vibrated by the vocal cords (i.e., voiced sound), while in other cases, the vocal cords do not vibrate during the formation of the sound (i.e., unvoiced sound). The mouth and its articulators (tongue, teeth, and lips) are then used to shape the airstream into a recognizable phone. Each phone bears a unique, articulatory signature. That letter and only that letter is sounded in this manner. In *A Practical Introduction to Phonetics*, Catford (1988) offers many illuminating insights on the nature and design of language. As an example, consider the phone /s/, as is Sam. While producing the /s/ sound, place the fingers on the front of the larynx (voice box). Now, without changing the shape of the mouth *at all*, convert the /s/ into a /z/, as in zipper. If done properly, you will notice a vibration in the throat that was not there before. This is the difference between an unvoiced phone (/s/) and a voiced phone (/z/). In the former, the vocal cords do not vibrate, while in the latter, they do. In actuality, this voicing is the *only* difference between these two sounds, all other articulators being oriented in exactly the same position in the mouth. There are many other examples similar to /s/ and /z/, such as /k/ and /g/, /p/ and /b/, and /t/ and /d/. For the convenience of the reader, in all cases the former phone in the pair is unvoiced, while the latter is voiced.

Returning to a discussion of the sixth column, the ancient linguists of Biblical Hebrew divided the letters into five phonetic classes. Moving from the back of the throat to the front of the mouth they are:

- **Guttural**-a sound produced deep in the throat
- **Palatal**-produced at the roof of the mouth (palate)
- **Lingual**-produced using the tongue
- **Dental**-produced at the teeth
- **Labial**-produced at the lips

One of the purposes of these articles will be to examine whether or not there is an association between the placement of a letter within the mouth (i.e., its articulation) and the meaning of the sound as it is used in the formation of language.

Finally, the seventh column sets out the specific astrological correspondences which will be used in these articles. This has already been discussed in a previous section, so I will not elaborate it further here.

Moving forward, then, the stage is now set to begin our analysis of the letters of the AHA, and to investigate the claim that there is a link between their sounds and meanings as employed in the formation of language.

ALEPH: GOD AND HIS QUALITIES

Aleph is the very first letter of the Ancient Hebrew Alefbayt (AHA), and therefore both literally and figuratively occupies a place of primacy in Biblical Hebrew (BH). It is both serially the first letter, as well as being the first of the three mother letters, which as will be exposed shortly, appear to provide a basic framework to the entire AHA. According to Kaplan (1997), phonetically, Aleph is classified by the Ancient Hebrew linguists as a guttural letter, pronounced deep in the back of the throat.

The three Mother letters of the AHA are linguistically distinct in meaningful ways. Aleph, which is typically associated with the ethereal concepts of God and spirit, is a guttural consonant, pronounced *invisibly* deep in the back of the throat. Maym, which is typically associated with the mundane constructs of physicality and matter, is a labial consonant, being pronounced *very visibly* at the front of the mouth by closing the lips completely. Hence, linguistically as well as figuratively, Maym is the exact opposite of Aleph. Aleph is a deep, back phone, while Maym is a high, front phone. Finally, consider that Shin the final Mother letter, is a phone produced intermediately within the vocal tract, being defined by the Ancient Kabbalists as a dental consonant, sounded by forming a passageway between the back and front of the mouth, which can be taken to represent a bridge between the invisible and visible worlds represented by Aleph and Maym, respectively. For this reason, metaphorically, the letter Shin is associated with the bridge between spirit and matter: the mind. Therefore, in the 3 mother letters, we have a framework that underpins the overall design of the Ancient Hebrew Alefbayt: we have yet another trinity that represents spirit, matter, and mind. Additionally, we have what appears to be a deliberate effort to transonify (i.e., to convert into sound) the universal concepts represented by these archetypes. This is a deeply profound effort on the part of the originators of the AHA, and is worthy of intense, continued study, until all the intentions of such an effort have been completely and appropriately parsed out.

In its form, א is said to be composed of three letters: a Yud above (י), a Yud below (י), and a Vav (ו) between them. Munk (1983) insightfully shares that the Yud above can be taken to be the spirit, the Yud below represents the physical world, and the Vav between them acts as the mind which connects and interfaces them. He also explains that the gematria of these three letters totals to 26, which is the same value as the Holy Name of God, יהוה. Hence, Munk (1983) and other Kabbalists draw a parallel between Aleph as the first letter of the AHA, and God as the first Force which motivates and creates the cosmos.

According to its serial gematria, Aleph is associated with the number 1, and hence denotes unity. This appears to further reinforce the monotheistic basis of the Jewish religion, which of course, has also come down to Christianity and Islam. Additionally, as Munk (1983) points out, through its association with the word "Aluph", which is consonantally spelled in exactly the same manner as Aleph (the only difference being the vowel sound), Aleph is associated with leadership, power, and strength.

Through my own linguistic studies, many of these reputed associations have been validated. However, additional insights have come to bear. Several words which begin with Aleph also refer, almost paradoxically, to darkness, duskiness, chaos, the void, nothingness, and the end. While it is an informed speculation, this association could be linked to the state of chaos and nothingness which began the world, and out of which the world was formed, from the Hebraic perspective. The fact that it also signifies an ending can also be understood according to the Judaic mindset, in that it is a common theme of Judeo-Christian myth that every beginning is an end, and every ending a new beginning.

Other qualities of God which are evinced by a linguistic study of the letter Aleph include a connection to words that mean "to exist", "bright, shining, fire, flame, or light", and "to be straight, right, happy, true, and good". This further supports the original statement that Aleph is effectively regarded as an attestation to God and God's Qualities.

Bayt: Bursting into Being

The first letter of the Alefbayt (AB) is Aleph. Yet, the first letter of the Torah, the sacred book of the Kabbalists, is Bayt. Why might this be so? Many explanations have been offered, all wonderful and complementary. One of my favorites is that Aleph represents the immaterial Spirit of God, while Bayt, as the second letter of the AB, represents the process of *b*irth, of *b*ursting forth into *b*eing which is accomplished by even the very first stroke of the Torah. Taken another way, here again we are admonished to always bear in mind that the presence and spirit of God was, is, and always will be supernal and undefinable. In the same way that the Judeo-Christian prohibition against creating idols reminds us that God is, in Its essence, beyond male, female, black, white, or any other descriptor, beginning the Torah with Bayt as opposed to Aleph reminds us of the infinite, immeasurable nature of the Supreme Being.

The Hebrew word Bayt means "house". This keyword hints at one of its many meanings. A house is the warm, protective, nurturing environment in which parents seek to raise and nourish their children. Similarly, the universe is the house, or the physical location, in which God seeks to raise and nourish us as so many offspring. Hence, Bayt, in a sense similar to the second mother letter, Maym, represents the physical or material world through which spirit seeks to express itself, develop, and grow.

From a linguistic point of view, it is not at all surprising that parallels can be drawn between Maym and Bayt. Maym is the second mother letter, while Bayt is the second serial letter of the AB. Linguistically, both letters are found in the same category, namely as labial consonants, meaning that in order to sound them, the airstream must be completely *b*locked by pursing the lips and then allowing it to *b*urst forth past the *b*arrier of the lips, giving *b*irth to the formation of a *b*arrage of sound. Perhaps I am *b*eing a bit poetic, but I hope the point will be made. Indeed, Magnus (2000) has completed a thorough and fascinating analysis of the phonemes in English, and has demonstrated compelling evidence that the relationship between sound and meaning is anything but random. That is, whether unconsciously or consciously, people appear to associate certain sounds with certain meanings. Forceful, *b*ursting phonemes, such as /b/, are used with far greater frequency in words that symbolize breaking through, breezing about, or some other sudden, forceful event. *It is as if the language is attempting to capture the meaning of the word through a linguistic approximation of its sonic value.* *S*ofter, *s*ubtler *s*ounds such as /s/ are used to describe *s*mooth, *s*weet, or even *s*ultry things. Unfortunately for our present studies, Magnus chose to perform her research in English rather than Biblical Hebrew. It would indeed be a thoroughly interesting study to see if such similarities of sound symbolism also exist in the latter.

Rabbi Michael Munk (1983) provides a thoroughly illuminating description of each of the Hebrew letters in his text *The Wisdom in the Hebrew Alphabet*, which is built upon his lifetime of research and investigation into the Hebrew culture and language. A recurrent theme in Rabbi Munk's analysis of the letter Bayt is the principle of duality. It is quite apparent where this link might come from, as Bayt is the second letter of the AB, and even as it is a bilabial consonant. Munk sees in the duality of Bayt a chance to reconcile the opposites upon which the world is constructed. In the Judeo-Christian conception, God begins as a Transcendent Unity which, in its desire to create the world, must divide into duality. This creates the world of opposites: light and dark, white and black, man and woman. However, opposites always beget a state of separation and polarity. It is through the symbolism of the Triad that the principle of harmony is introduced: opposites in balance, which thereby create a sustainable, healthful equilibrium which can form and foster life. The duality symbolized by Bayt is a critical step in this movement from the unmanifest to the manifest. It does not complete the quest, but without it, the quest fails.

GIMEL: HARMONY AND STRENGTH

The third letter of the Alefbayt (AB) is Gimel, reconciler of paradoxes. Aleph represents the archetype of spirit; that which is invisible, unknowable, and entirely beyond definition or description. Bayt symbolizes the archetype of matter; that which is visible, knowable, and clearly delineated, but devoid of animation. The third letter of the Ancient Hebrew Alphabet (AHA), Gimel, bridges the seemingly untraversable chasm between these two extremes, through the mediator of mind. It provides a point of contact between the spirit which animates our existence and the physical world which is animated by it.

The principle of harmony stands at the crossroads of our existence. While there are many important concepts in spirituality and in life, the principle of harmony is chief among them. Harmony rules our lives and bodies. Harmony in the body leads to health, and the loss of it engenders disease. Harmony in our marriages leads to bliss, while disharmony leads to disaster. It is fair to say that while our current society stresses a state of "more is better" or "bigger is better", it is decidedly not so in the human body. Any point of extremism, whether towards excess or paucity, ultimately ends in illness. If we eat too little, we become emaciated and weak. If we eat too much, we become overburdened with weight, joint issues, higher risks of cardiovascular disease and cancer, as well as a whole host of additional diseases. The state of harmony achieves health in the body, while carelessly careening towards disequilibrium feeds disease states. This principle appears to apply blanketly across life- not just in the human body, but in all matters.

Linguistically, true to its form, the sound /g/ is produced in the center of the vocal tract. Aleph is produced as a guttural deep in the throat in its invisible realms, while Maym is produced in full view at the lips, in the same way that spirit and matter are respectively covert and overt. Gimel, like the third mother letter, Shin, is formed in the middle of the vocal tract, phonetically bridging the gap between the two extremes of sound production. Specifically, in *Sefer Yetzirah*, Aryeh Kaplan (1997) explains that the ancient Kabbalists regarded Gimel as a palatal, formed at the roof of the mouth where the hard and soft palate meet. It is one of seven double letters, therefore bearing two distinct pronunciations. In its astrological correspondence, it is associated with Jupiter, the planet of greatness, wealth, and good fortune. Indeed, the Hebrew word *gadol* means "great" while *gibor* means "mighty". *Gevurah* is indicative of power, also doubling as one of only ten Sefirot in the Kabbalistic Tree of Life. It is not hard to see why; enunciating the letter brings a forceful cone of expulsion, reverberating the air with strength and power. Perhaps it is not at all by accident that our own word for Divinity, God, also begins with this letter of balance, proportion, and power.

Dalet: Born into Being

The fourth letter of the Ancient Hebrew Alefbayt (AHA) is Dalet, which translates as "door". It is indeed a door, if not *the* door through which all manifestation occurs. The number 4 is of incredible value and import in Sacred Geometry, as explained in detail in the earlier article on the Tetrad. This same import is reiterated in Kabbalistic literature. As described by Kaplan (1997) in *Sefer Yetzirah*, Kabbalists refer to the Four Worlds, through which all existence is made possible. The first world is Azilut, or Emanation. This is the spiritual level where an idea is first conceived. The second world is Beriah, or Creation. This is the level at which a mental picture of the idea is formed. The third world, Yetzirah, or Formation, represents the commitment of energy and emotion to the realization of the idea. Finally, in the fourth step that desire is brought into being, through the world of Assiyah, or Action. This last world represents the manifestation of the goal in reality.

It is not at all accidental that those in the Brotherhood of Light tradition apply a similar concept, though the symbolism of the four elements is employed. In the Brotherhood of Light's schema, Fire represents the first world, Air the second, Water the third, and Earth the fourth. Indeed, these are abiding and memorable teachings, lodging themselves deep in the consciousness of the learner.

The same precept is communicated arithmetically in the seemingly elementary, yet clandestinely profound, equation: $1 + 2 + 3 + 4 = 10$. In this formula, a similar principle of a fourfold process of manifestation is revealed. It depicts mathematically the belief of the ancient mathematical philosophers that it requires no less than four discrete stages to complete a cycle (as represented by the Decad). This equation may well form the basis for our entire system of mathematics, as has been discussed at length in the earlier articles on the Tetrad and Decad.

Finally, the same formula is observed geometrically in the famed Tetrakys of Pythagoras, an ancient visual representation of the inextricable link between 4 and 10 (see below).

The Tetrakys is at once four (serially) and ten (cumulatively). It demonstrates pictographically the enduring link between the Tetrad as a symbol of an idea brought into being through four discrete stages, and the Decad as the symbol of the completion of a cycle of manifestation.

Linguistically, Dalet is classified by the ancient Kabbalists as a lingual, indicating that it is formed with the tongue. According to Burton, Dechaine, and Vatikiotis-Bateson (2012, p.42), modern linguistics classifies /d/ as a "voiced alveolar stop", which describes the placement of the tongue in its articulation as just behind the teeth at a portion of the mouth called the alveolar ridge. From my own observations and investigations, I believe that the tongue, in making the sound /d/, moves *d*ownward, *d*eepening, *d*arkening tone, and perhaps even *d*ying to its former high place. Whether through its motion or its association with the planet Mars, it begins the words for death, destruction, disease, damage, and a whole host of other words which indicate dismay. Magnus (2000) has performed extensive research on the relationship between sound and meaning in the English language, and many of these musings are authenticated by her work.

Hence, in the letter Dalet, we discover a letter which simultaneously represents death and life, an ending and a new beginning. To some readers, this might seem paradoxical, but if one is familiar with the concepts promulgated by the ancient Kabbalists, then it could *only* be this way, as they witnessed in every ending a new beginning, and observed in every death a presage to a new life.

HE: BREATH & LIFE

The fifth letter of the Alefbayt (AB) is the letter He (pronounced "hay"). According to Burton, Dechaine, and Vatikiotis-Bateson (2012), He is classified by modern linguistics as a *voiceless glottal fricative*, indicating that it is produced deep in the throat, without the vibration of the vocal cords, and that the air is made turbulent through the partial contraction of the glottis. The ancient classification is not that different, being described by the Kabbalists as a *guttural* consonant (Kaplan, 1997). The sound He is essentially an audible breath, and this description coincides well not only with its physical description, but also with its esoteric meaning.

The fifth letter, He, shares much in common symbolically with the Pentad, the fifth number. The hallmark of the Pentad, whether considered geometrically as a pentagon or a pentagram, is that it is *self-replicating*. That is, pentagons and pentagrams can be inscribed or circumscribed infinitely within or without each other (see Figure 1 below). The ability to reproduce more of oneself is a basic hallmark of life. Hence, the Pentad is also symbolic of the human life which is possible only through the breath.

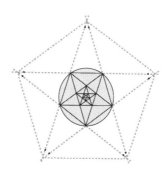

Figure 1: Pentagrams can be inscribed within pentagrams endlessly.

This symbolism of breath and life is reinforced in several interesting ways. First of all, He is the first elemental letter of the Alefbayt, and therefore corresponds to the first sign of the Zodiac, Aries. Aries is also the sign of life, the beginning of all things, the very first quintessence which distills down as the mystery behind being.

The Kabbalists give further support to the association between He and life in their description of the constitution of a living thing. The first four elements (i.e., fire, air, water, earth) are said to make up the physical constitution of an organism, in that it takes no less than four discrete steps to move from a state of nothingness to a *physically* manifest being. However, a body without life, without breath, is inanimate. The fifth element, **ether**, representative of energy, is what vivifies the physical body. It is only through the introduction of the breath, the spiritual animation of life, that existence becomes possible, and that living things develop, with their unique ability to adapt and respond to their environment.

Very interestingly, the pentagram and pentagon are loaded with examples of the Golden Ratio, yet another sign and hallmark of living things. The Golden Ratio is not a number, but rather a relationship between numbers which also has the quality of being replicable at infinitely smaller and larger scales (see Figure 2 below). The Golden Ratio is found clandestinely all over nature, for example in the shell of a nautilus, the path of a hurricane, or even the shape of a galaxy (see Figure 3 below)

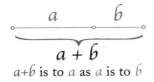

$a+b$ is to a as a is to b

 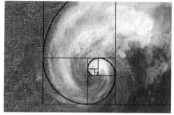

Figure 2: A line bisected according to the Golden Section.

Figure 3: Some examples of the Golden Ratio in nature

What's more, the proportions of the human body are also replete with the significance of the Golden Ratio, or phi, as it is currently called (see image 4 below). It seems that wherever life exists, phi also can be discovered.

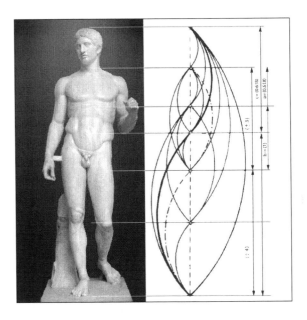

Figure 4: An example of Phi (the Golden Ratio) in the human body

It would be a curious study indeed to investigate all the myriad ways in which the sound He represents and links to other symbols associated with life, such as phi. Is He somehow a phonological representation of the Golden Ratio? Is there a relationship between the lengths of the two distinct sounds (/h/ and /e/) which make it up? Just how far does the common symbolism of He and phi extend?

For now, it is very fair to say that the fifth letter of the Ancient Hebrew Alefbayt (AHA) is the subtle sound of the breath as it enters or exits the human body. As all other gutturals, it is produced mysteriously out of sight, and for this reason is associated more with the hidden nature of spirit than with the physical body. It is the sound of life itself, for if the body is devoid of breath, it is also bereft of life.

Waw: Symmetry & Physical Perfection

The sixth letter of the Alefbayt (AB) is the sacred sound Waw. Many people will know this letter by its more common modern name, "Vav". However, it is crucial in our treatment of this letter from a phonosemantic point of view to make a correction right away.

Garrett (2008) reveals that while the modern pronunciation of the sixth letter of the Alefbayt is Vav, in biblical times it was instead pronounced Waw. Furthermore, Kaplan (1997) identifies the sixth letter of the Ancient Hebrew Alefbayt (AHA) as a *labial*, which is to say that it is pronounced at the lips. Other letters which share this classification include Maym, Pay, and Bayt. The hallmark of labial consonants is that they involve the use of the lips to articulate the sound. By contrast, "Vav", if it were pronounced as such, would be Kabbalistically classified as a *dental*, which is a group of letters that anciently were considered to use the teeth to produce a sound. Other members of this articulatory group include Shin, Samech, Zayin, and Tzaddi. While it may seem like a small point from a grammatic point of view, from a phonosemantic point of view, the two belong to entirely different articulatory classes, and therefore carry different phonosemantic symbolisms.. As our proposition is that there is a meaning and value attached to each letter based on its sound, it would be grossly in error not to address this discrepancy immediately.

In my own investigations, having first analyzed the numbers of the Decad through the lens of Sacred Geometry, and then turned my attention to the letters of the Alefbayt, I have observed tremendous commonality between the symbolisms of the letters and the numbers of the same serial value within the AHA. For example, there was great semantic similarity between the Pentad and He, the fifth number and letter of the Alefbayt, respectively. The same principle has generally held true for all letters and numbers analyzed thus far. Indeed, it has functioned at times as a light in the darkness of alphabetic interpretation.

In this vein, I have investigated the sixth letter of the AB from a phonetic as well as a mathematic point of view. In the field of Sacred Geometry, the Hexad represents perfection of form, and this is also a theme of the letter Waw. The letter itself is symmetric, or at least it was in its earliest form: Υ, when it was quite literally a pictograph of a tent stake, as its name "hook" or "peg" connotes (Benner, 2019). But the ancient Kabbalists had a gift for seeing the divine in the mundane, and it would be an insulting underestimation of their genius to assume that simply because this letter started out as representing the very mundane, even banal tent stake, that their interpretation and value of the object stopped at a purely literal level. As we have observed again and again in our studies thus far, every object, no matter how mundane, had a deeper, hidden, spiritual value to them. Indeed, it may well be this esoteric spiritual meaning which implores us to continue to investigate their alphabetic structure so many centuries later.

Beyond the physical symmetry of the sixth letter as originally written in Ancient Hebrew, its name, Waw, is also palindromic, demonstrating an uncanny written and enunciated symmetry. *That is, when Waw is pronounced, it also produces a perfectly symmetric articulation in the vocal tract.* The lips are first pursed, then the mouth is extended to permit the vowel, and then the lips are once again pursed to complete the word. Therefore, in the very pronunciation of the letter, as in its original written AHA form as well as the scripting of its name, one of the recurrent themes of the letter Waw is **Symmetry**.

Other examples of the connection between the number six and the concept of symmetry and perfection of physical form abound. As Munk (1983, p.94) relates, "The physical world was completed in six days and a complete self-contained object consists of six dimensions: above and below, right and left, before and behind...the census of the Jewish Nation was 600,000, corresponding to the 600,000 letters in the Torah."

There are compelling mathematic reasons why the number six may be so strongly associated with symmetry and perfection of form. First and most simply, any object which occupies physical space must have exactly three dimensions: length, width, and breadth. If we imagine a line moving off towards infinity in either direction for each of these three dimensions, then that will create exactly six directions of physical space (see below).

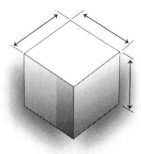

Cube demonstrating how the three dimensions of space yield six directions.

Furthermore, as described by Iamblicus (1988), Nicomachus of Gerasa (2015), Schneider (1994), and Taylor (1816), the number six is the *first perfect number*, i.e., a number that is equal to the sum of its factors. To state this mathematically, 1 + 2 + 3 = 6. However, the number six has other, even more peculiar properties. It is also one of the very few numbers that is equal to the product of its factors: 1 x 2 x 3 = 6. Since it is equal to its factors additively and multiplicatively, it can also be treated intriguingly with the opposite operations, namely subtraction and division, respectively: 6 − 3 − 2 = 1 and 6 ÷ 3 ÷ 2 = 1. Therefore, the number six demonstrates fascinating properties of equality and symmetry. This may be why the Kabbalists of old so strongly associated it with the concept of physical perfection and symmetry.

Zayin: The Light in the Darkness

The seventh letter of the Ancient Hebrew Alefbayt (AHA) is Zayin. Through its association with the Heptad, as well as by virtue of its name alone, *Zayin symbolizes the presence of the divine within the seemingly ordinary, mundane world of daily existence*. It also bespeaks a deep and penetrating form of harmony which differs in its structure and function from those associated with the Triad or Pentad.

As Schneider (1994, p. 224) relates, of all the numbers within the Decad, the one which is said to be most similar to the perfect Monad, symbol of God and the source of all things, is the Heptad. Like the Monad, it was called "virgin", in the sense that no other number within the Decad enters into it evenly (e.g., as 2 enters 4, or 3 enters 6). It is also called "childless", in that the Heptad cannot produce any other number within the Decad through multiplication (as 2 produces 4, or 3 produces 6 and 9). Additionally, neither 1 nor 7 can be expressed as a product of any two whole numbers except for itself and 1 (i.e., they are prime). Finally, of all the quantities between 1 and 9, *the Heptad is the only number which cannot divide 360 evenly, the number of degrees in a circle*. Hence, while it is possible to draw exactly polygons based on every other single digit, it is never possible to draw a perfect heptagon. The ancients took this as an eternal reminder of the presence of the innumerable, innominable, indescribable spirit which animates matter- omnipresent, eternal, elusive, and yet in many senses, more real that the transient, mutable, world it enlivens. They saw in the Heptad the light in the darkness; a flame illuminating the pure, spiritual state which vivifies and perpetuates the physical world, but which can never be completely replicated by it.

Analyzing the name Zayin phonosemantically reveals a similar insight. In Hebrew, the word Zayin is composed of three consonants: Zayin (Z), Yud (Y), and Nun (N). *Notice that Yud hides between the other two letters.* Numerically, Yud has a gematria of 10, which reduces to 1, the number of the Creator of All Things (10 →1 + 0 = 1). Here again, we see built into the very name of the letter itself a reminder of the eternal presence of the divine within the mundane.

Phonosemantic analysis also reveals further insights. In the Ancient Hebrew classification system, the /z/ of Zayin is a dental, indicating that it is articulated using the teeth. Other letters in this class include Shin, Tzaddi, and Samech. If you listen as you sound them, you will hear that they all involve the forceful flow of air through a small channel in the mouth. According to modern linguistics, these sounds are known as *fricatives*, owing to the significant turbulence which is produced when they are sounded (Burton, Dechaine, & Vatikiotis-Bateson, 2012). In terms of the three mother letters, then, this puts Zayin in closest phonological relationship with Shin, as they are both dentals. In fact, very interestingly, as explained by Catford (1988), there is *no difference whatsoever* in the articulatory postures of the various structures of the vocal tract between the /s/ of Shin and the /z/ of Zayin. The only distinction between them is that /s/ is unvoiced, while /z/ is voiced. These are linguistic terms which refer to whether or not the vocal cords vibrate as the letter is produced.

As described in detail by Catford (1988), you can perform a fun little experiment to verify this for yourself. Place your thumb and forefinger lightly on your voicebox and hum. You will feel the vibration of the vocal cords as you do so. This is referred to linguistically as *voicing*. Next, stop humming. You can feel that the vocal cords have stopped moving. This is referred to linguistically as an *unvoiced* sound. Do this a few times to get used to the feeling of *voiced* and *unvoiced* sounds, respectively. With a little effort, you can develop the ability to deliberately turn voicing on or off at will, which simply amounts to whether or not the vocal folds vibrate when a phone is being sounded. A consonant is considered *voiced* if the vocal cords vibrate while it is being sounded, and it is considered *unvoiced* if the vocal cords do not vibrate while it is being sounded. /s/ is an unvoiced consonant, while /z/ is a voiced consonant. With this background knowledge in place, we can now move onto the second part of the experiment.

Place your thumb and forefinger lightly on your voicebox again and create a continuous /s/ sound. You will notice that there is no vibration coming from your vocal cords. This is why /s/ is considered an unvoiced consonant; there is no vibration necessary at the vocal cords to produce it. *Now, while maintaining your fingers on your voicebox, without changing anything whatsoever about the shape of your mouth, introduce the humming sound of the vocal folds (i.e., voicing).* What happened to the sound?

You probably noticed that the /s/ sound changed into a /z/ sound. In fact, the *only* difference between these two phones is that /s/ is unvoiced, while /z/ is voiced. Nothing else about the mouth, tongue, teeth, or lips (i.e., articulators) has to change to alternate between these two sounds. Pretty neat, huh? There are several other letter pairs like this, such as /p/ and /b/, /f/ and /v/, /t/ and /d/, and /k/ and /g/, where the only difference between them is whether they are unvoiced or voiced, respectively. You can try these out, too, by applying the same method. Returning to our discussion of Zayin, according to Kaplan (1997) ancient Kabbalists regarded the /z/ of Zayin as a dental consonant. As a dental, it falls into a group of Hebrew letters including Tzaddi,

Samech, and most importantly, Shin. Shin is a mother letter, and forms one of the three basic archetypes upon which the AHA is based. It is the third and final mother letter, and is therefore associated with the Triad, or the principle of harmony. But what possible form of harmony could stem from the Heptad? Well, probably the form of harmony you are most familiar with: musical harmony.

Schneider (1994) explains in tremendous and fascinating detail the legend of the monochord and the subsequent discovery of the Western musical scale by Pythagoras. You can re-create this intriguing experiment if you have a stringed instrument lying around (for this purposes, an unfretted instrument will work best, but any stringed instrument will work). Begin by plucking any open string. It will produce a certain tone, based on its length and thickness. This represents the Monad, or the basic fundamental unit of our investigation.

Now place your finger exactly in the middle of the string and pluck half its length. If you are in the exact center, you will notice that the same tone is produced, only one register higher. As the string is being divided in two, this action represents the introduction of the Dyad. And just as the Monad and Dyad give rise to all other numbers, all of the infinite possible musical tones are encompassed within the limits defined by the full string and half string.

Music would be quite boring indeed, though, if all we did was pluck a string in its full and half length. But how can we move forward to introduce new tones to the musical scale, while still retaining the underlying principle of harmony? For that, we will need to introduce the Triad. In order to do so, divide the string *unequally* in such a way that the long part of the string produces the same tone as the short part of the string. Doing so reveals that the string will be divided into 1/3 and 2/3 portions, and the note that will be produced is what is termed in music the fifth. This explains why the fifth is such an important musical interval, and even why it is termed perfect. *It is not a forced imposition of sound on the string, but rather a natural harmony which emanates from it.* Therefore, it stands in perfect relationship to the original tone produced by the full and half string.

If we then take the 2/3 section of the string as our new length, and proceed to derive a 2/3 length of that new length, performing this action iteratively, we will arrive at the foundational "circle of fifths". After exactly *seven* such divisions, the original tone repeats, only one half-tone higher (e.g., C becomes C#). After exactly *twelve* such divisions, the musical scale comes back on itself, and the original tone is reproduced. By finally taking all of the natural harmonies so produced, and clustering them into one octave, the modern day diatonic (7 tone) and chromatic (12 tone) scales are born.

Hence, Zayin, the seventh letter of the Ancient Hebrew Alefbayt serves as a light in the darkness, an eternal reminder of the presence of the spiritual within the material. Additionally, it describes the basis for what has come to be known as the "music of the spheres"- a musical scale which is based on the natural, innate harmonies of a simple string vibrating with limitless capacities.

CHAYT: DEATH & REBIRTH

The eighth letter of the Ancient Hebrew Alefbayt (AHA) is Chayt. According to Kaplan (1997), the Hebrew meaning of this word is "fence", and it is an apt moniker. Much as its role in music (i.e., the octave), the Octad stands at the crossroads between the completion, or death, of one cycle, and the initiation, or rebirth, of the next cycle. In this sense, paradoxically it can be associated equally well with death and renewed life.

As Munk (1983) details, this is reflected linguistically in the fact that the Hebrew word for sin, Chayt, begins with this letter. Sin is a sort of metaphorical death, in that actions taken against the Will of God distance the actor from God, the ultimate source of Life, Light, and Love. However, much as the repentant sinner is forgiven and reintegrates into his or her spiritual community, the correction of wrongful actions leads to a deeper, richer celebration of life. Interestingly, the Hebrew word for life, Chaim, also begins with Chayt, indicating that it is only through the metaphorical death to a lower level of existence that a higher order of being becomes possible.

Kaplan (1997) relates that Chayt is classified as a guttural linguistically, which places it in closest relationship with the mother letter, Aleph. Recall that as the first letter of the entire AHA, Aleph symbolizes the Creative Force of God. However, in the case of Chayt, the principle is not so much creation as *re-creation*. Hence, Chayt represents the dissolution of the old system, followed by the triumphant re-birth of a new level of expression.

The symbolism of death and re-birth is strikingly and fastidiously retained in the structure of the word "Chayt" itself. The Hebrew word "Chayt" is composed of three letters: Chayt, Yud, and Tav. Chayt is a fricative, guttural sound. It has no English equivalent, but is rather pronounced as the "ch" in the German word "Bach". The sound is turbulent and disorganized, and is therefore well representative of the disorganization and chaos which results from dissolution and death. The second letter, Yud, is the tenth letter of the AHA, and therefore well represents the rebirth of a new level of action. In fact, there is perhaps no greater representation of the movement from one plane to the next than the Decad (10), in that the number itself is composed of the number of beginnings, the Monad (1), as well as a 0, in this case indicating the completion of one round of activity. Finally, the third letter that comprises the word Chayt is Tav, the final letter of the entire AHA, which further reinforces the concept of Chayt as both an ending and a new beginning.

As the eighth letter of the AHA, Chayt is also strongly associated with the Octad. Schneider (1994, p. 268) communicates that anciently the Octad was known as "promiscuous", in direct contrast to its neighbor, the Heptad, in that it has more divisors than any other number in the Decad (i.e., 1, 2, 4). It was also called "justice", as it is an "evenly even" number, in that it can be halved all the way down to unity (i.e., $8/2 = 4$; $4/2 = 2$; $2/2 = 1$). Furthermore, the Octad is the only number besides the Monad composed of three identical divisors ($8 = 2 \times 2 \times 2$) making it the only other cubed number in the Decad. For these reasons, it was also known as "mother" owing to its strong associations with the material world of substance and form.

Of all of these various epithets, the one that connects most directly with the symbolism of the Hebrew letter Chayt appears to be "justice", as the latter is so often seen as a weighing in of all forces involved, an impartial reckoning and accounting of all possible factors. Justice implies an arrival at a point of equilibrium, the establishment of a point of agreement where all old factors have been taken into account, and a new course has been charted. In much the same way that the Octad stands at the crossroads between an old cycle that is falling away and a new one that is just beginning, the eighth letter of the AHA, Chayt, represents a transition point between that which was and that which will be.

TAYT: THE HARMONY OF HARMONIES

The ninth letter of the Hebrew Alefbayt (AB) is Tayt, and as seems to have become the pattern, it is closely aligned with the symbolism of the Ennead. The Ennead is the highest single digit, and represents the climax and completion of the journey which began with the Monad. The Monad represents the first impulse of an idea, which then moves through a process of growth and development, ultimately culminating in the realization of that idea through the Ennead.

As Schneider details (1994), the Ennead can also be considered a *trinity of trinities*, in that it is composed of 3 x 3. *As such, it represents a state of harmony and balance on the spiritual, physical, and mental planes.* Just as the Triad, of which the Ennead is a multiple, represented a state of balance between the Monad and Dyad, the Ennead expresses the same notion of balance, in this case applied to all three triads between the monad and ennead. In this sense, if we logically extend the pattern established by the initial three archetypes, we proceed from the Spiritual Plane (Monad), to the Physical Plane (Dyad), through the bridge of the Mental Plane (Triad). Logically, then, it would seem that the First Triad (i.e., Monad, Dyad, Triad) pertains to the spiritual dimension, the Second Triad (Tetrad, Pentad, Hexad) relates to the physical dimension, and the Third Triad (Heptad, Octad, Ennead) comprehends the mental dimension.

The Ennead occupies a singular and even spectacular position as *the harmony of harmonies.* Not only it is a harmony within the Third Triad which relates to mind (i.e., a balance point between the Heptad and Octad), but it is also a point of equilibrium between the other Triads within the Decad. Even more astonishingly, this design of nested harmonies is reflected linguistically in the point of articulation of the letter associated with the Ennead, Tayt.

Kaplan (1997) relates that in the Kabbalistic system, Tayt is classified as a lingual. This is to say that the letter is formed through the use of the tongue. Of the 5 points of articulation expounded by the ancient Kabbalists (i.e, guttural, palatal, lingual, dental, and labial), lingual consonants are quite literally the most central sounds produced within the human vocal tract. This coincides well with the conception of Tayt as representative of a state of balance, harmony, and order produced through the resolution of opposites.

Still more amazing is the fact that the sound Tayt not only occupies a point of centrality when considered solely according to its linguistic classification as a lingual, but also occupies a point of harmony against all the other points of harmony within the Decad. That is to say, Tayt occupies a point of harmony between Gimel (a palatal consonant, representative of the Triad), and Waw (a labial consonant, representative of the Hexad). Thus, linguistically Tayt is quite literally a harmony of harmonies; not only in its placement in number, but also in its point of articulation within the vocal tract! Perhaps the table on the following page will help to clarify my meaning:

Letter Grouping	First Position in Triad	Second Position in Triad	Third Position in Triad	Third Position is a Point of Compromise between First and Second Positions?
Mother	Aleph (guttural)	Maym (labial)	Shin (dental)	Y
Spiritual Triad	Aleph (guttural)	Bayt (labial)	Gimel (palatal)	Y
Physical Triad	Dalet (lingual)	Heh (guttural)	Waw (labial)	N
Mental Triad	Zayin (dental)	Chet (guttural)	Tayt(lingual)	Y
Triad of Triads (3, 6, 9)	Gimel (palatal)	Waw (labial)	Tayt (lingual)	Y

In 4 of the 5 classes described in the table above, the articulation of the third letter in the triad occupies a position which is intermediate to the points of articulation of the first two letters. Not only does this occur in the Mother Letter Triad, the Spiritual Triad, and the Mental Triad, but it is even true when we consider a triad of triads, inclusive of the numbers 3, 6, and 9, as the natural triads which occur within the Decad.

Yod: Multiplicity as Unity

Munk (1983) describes beautifully that the tenth letter of the Ancient Hebrew Alefbayt (AHA), Yod, is the smallest of all the letters, indicating that as with the Monad, it is a seed of things to come. It is also the only letter that hangs suspended above the written line, representative of a new plane of action and endeavor, for it is the first letter associated with a double digit number, indicating a movement beyond the original archetypes symbolized by the nine single digits.

Perhaps the simplest way to penetrate the symbolism of Yod is by way of its association with the Decad (10). The notation of the number 10 perfectly captures its intent: as comprised of 1 and 0, it is a unity formed through multiplicity. It acts as both an ending and a beginning. It is both old and new at once. It exists at a perfect point of balance, poised between two planes.

Linguistically, Yod bears an uncanny sonic resemblance to its notation in number. The letter /y/ is classified by modern linguistics as a *"palatal approximant"* (Burton, Dechaine, & Vatiki-otis-Bateson, 2012, p. 45). This describes the fact that the letter is sounded by partially restricting the air flow through the vocal tract, with the center of the tongue raised close to the palate. Unlike a consonant, however, the airflow is never completely obstructed, hence it cannot be called a true consonant. On the other hand, air is not allowed to flow freely as in the case of a true vowel. For this reason, /y/ can act either as a vowel or consonant in language, depending on its position and use, a function which has earned it the epithet *"semi-vowel"*.

While this is not always the case, the modern classification of the letter /y/ concurs with that of the ancient Kabbalists (Kaplan, 1997). They also classified this letter as a *palatal*, indicating its point of articulation within the vocal tract. Recall that the ancient Kabbalists defined five points of articulation in the mouth: gutturals, palatals, linguals, dentals, and labials. The deepest points of articulation coincide with letters that pertain to the spiritual world, while the more overt points of articulation correspond to the material word. As a palatal, Yod acts as a bridge between the spiritual and material, while still reminding us of its primarily spiritual origins through its closer proximity to the deepest recesses of the vocal tract.

Interestingly, if you slow down the phonation of the letter /y/ you will discover that it is actually a glide of two distinct vowel sounds: /i/ and /a/. Recall that /a/, as the first letter of the AHA, is the phonic representation of the Monad. Once again, we are reminded of Yod's implicit link to unity. On the other hand, whereas Aleph represented a pure and initiating singularity, Yod represents a unity born through multiplicity, and thereby bears a second symbol, 0, in its representation. Phonically, this completed cycle might be represented by the /i/ sound of /y/, a high, front vowel, representing well the now manifest Decad. Taken according to this interpretation, the sound /y/ is the literal transonfication of the number 10.

Whatever its sound symbolism, it is clear that through its position as a pivot point between single and compound numbers, the tenth letter, Yod, acts as a bridge between that which has been and that which wishes to be. It stands at the boundary between past and future, and in this sense, represents the *infinite present*, in which all manifestation and manner of action exists.

KAPH: MOVING TOWARDS
MANIFESTATION

The eleventh letter of the Ancient Hebrew Alefbayt (AHA) is Kaph. According to Burton, Dechaine, & Vatikiotis-Bateson (2012, p. 42), in modern linguistics /k/ is classified as a "*voiceless velar stop*", as it is pronounced by momentarily interrupting the air flow near the velum, or soft palate. As related by Kaplan (1997), the Kabbalists used a different name, but similarly defined the point of articulation of /k/ as a *palatal*, indicating that it is articulated by interrupting airflow at the palate, or roof of the mouth.

Recall once more that the Kabbalists identified 5 distinct points of articulation in the vocal tract. Beginning from the most recessed position and moving toward the most overt, they are: guttural, palatal, lingual, dental, and labial. At the mid-way point of these explorations, while it is still too early to draw ultimate conclusions, it does indeed appear that there is a relationship between the point of articulation of a sound and its value in Biblical Hebrew (BH). Linguistically, this concept is called phonosemantics, and seeks to analyze the link between sound and meaning in the use of language. Applying this concept, guttural letters in the AHA, as they are produced in the most hidden and unseen portions of the vocal tract, are associated with the hidden, unseen nature of the world of spirit. By contrast, labial letters, which have their point of articulation as obviously and overtly as possible, are associated with the obvious, overt objects and constructs of the material universe. Consonants occupying an intermediate point of articulation, most specifically linguals, are associated with the bridge between spirit and matter, the mind, or mental plane of being.

From a phonosemantic point of view, Kaph, as a palatal

consonant, most closely resonates with the idea of *the movement from spirit to matter*. This symbolism is reinforced by its intermediate position as a palatal consonant, an analysis of the letters that constitute the letter name "Kaph", and a consideration of Kaph's gematria.

As a palatal, the letter Kaph is articulated at a point intermediate between gutturals, most closely associated with spirit, and linguals, which are strictly associated with the mind. Hence, in terms of sound symbolism, palatals appear to indicate a point of transition between the spiritual and mental planes of being. This idea is further reinforced by an analysis of the letter's name, Kaph. Unlike English, in Biblical Hebrew, each letter has a specific name. In the AHA, the letter name Kaph is comprised of /k/ and /ph/, with a short /a/ vowel in between. Analyzing the points of articulation of these distinct letters, we observe the letter /k/ originates at the palatal position, and then moves to /ph/, a labial consonant (In BH, /ph/ if formed by aspirating the letter /p/, which is a labial consonant). This sound symbolism is consistent with the idea of a letter indicating a transition from mind to matter. Finally, the gematria of Kaph in the AHA is 20, which resolves to 2 (i.e., 20 → 2 + 0 = 2), indicating a link with the Dyad, archetype of the material world. This further supports a primary association between the letter Kaph and the physical world. Taken together, in the AHA letter Kaph, we discover an apt symbol of the movement from spirit to matter, from the inception of an idea toward its ultimate realization.

LAMED: LORD OF LORDS

The twelfth letter of the Ancient Hebrew Alefbayt (AHA) is Lamed, which Munk (1983) relates stands at the exact center of the AHA, towering above all the other letters. Its height and central position communicate well the primacy of this letter's role in the AHA. *As denoted by its position and size, it communicates clearly the principles of balance, harmony, and centrality.* These principles are revealed in myriad ways.

The number 12 mathematically reduces to 3 ($12 \rightarrow 1 + 2 = 3$), the archetypal number associated with balance, harmony, and an equilibrium of forces. An analysis of the gematria of Lamed leads to an identical conclusion (i.e., $30 \rightarrow 3 + 0 = 3$). This principle of harmony and centrality is further demonstrated in the articulation and production of the sound Lamed itself. Linguistically, the Ancient Kabbalists classified Lamed as a *lingual*, indicating that it is produced through the use of the tongue. Of the five classes of consonants, namely gutturals, palatals, linguals, dentals, and labials, linguals occupy the most central position. As if to emphasize this conclusion still further, Kaplan's (1997, p. 102) *Sefer Yetzirah* reveals that Lamed is listed as the most centrally located of the lingual consonants:

Twenty-two foundation letters,
He engraved them with voice,
He carved them with breath,
He set them in the mouth in five places.
Alef, Chet, Heh, Eyin, in the throat,
Gimel, Yud, Kaf, Kuf, in the palate,
*Dalet, Tet, **Lamed**, Nun, Tav, in the tongue,*
Zayin, Samekh, Shin, Resh, Tzadi, in the teeth,
Bet, Vav, Mem, Peh, in the lips.

As in the AHA itself, in this passage from *Sefer Yetzirah*, Lamed resides at the exact center of the articulated consonants. A final indication of Lamed's centrality can be found in the fact that astrologically, it is associated with the sign Libra, yet another overt symbol of balance and centrality of position.

In *The Wisdom in the Hebrew Alphabet*, Munk (1983, p. 141) sagely reflects that the letter Lamed begins the Hebrew word "lev", which means "heart". Just as the letter Lamed resides at the exact middle of the AHA, the heart resides at the core of our being, distributing the nourishment and sustenance that animates life. Interestingly, Munk (1983) goes on the relate that the entire Torah is bounded by the two letters which comprise the word "lev", namely Lamed and Bayt (which, under certain conditions, is pronounced *Vayt* in Biblical Hebrew). The first letter of the Torah is Bayt, while the last letter of this sacred text is Lamed. It is as if the authors of the Torah wanted us to understand that the entire Torah, all of the laws and divinely inspired words of God, can reside in our own hearts, should we be pure and true seekers of wisdom. Additionally, we can take this as an admonition to make the words and teachings of the Torah the heart and core of our very being- not just words or prayers to chant mindlessly, but eternal, timeless principles to live by, in order to create our most authentic and true selves.

The letter Lamed clearly occupied a primary role in the minds of the ancient Kabbalists, and given its core tenets of balance, harmony, and centrality, we would also do well to assign it the same import in our own lives.

Maym: Manifestation and Matter

Maym is the thirteenth serial letter and the second mother letter of the Ancient Hebrew Alefbayt (AHA). Both symbolically and linguistically, it stands in direct contrast to Aleph, the first serial and mother letter. Symbolically, Aleph represents the invisible, unseen aspects of spirit, while Maym represents the visible grandeur of manifestation. Linguistically, the two letters and their associated sounds are completely contrary: Aleph is a deep, back consonant, classified by the AHA linguists as a *guttural*, while Maym is a high, front consonant, sounded by pursing the lips together to completely block the flow of air, and is for this reason classified as a *labial* consonant.

As Maym is the second mother letter, it bears a strong relationship to the Dyad, archetype of matter and physical substance. Through its strict Gematria of 4 (40 → 4 + 0 = 4; 13 → 1 + 3 = 4), the association of Maym with the physical world is further reinforced. Recall that in the most technical of terms, the Tetrad is the first truly even number, the Monad and Dyad being considered rather as the parents of number (Taylor, 1816). According to the same author, odd numbers were anciently conceptualized as masculine through their association with the Monad, while even numbers were regarded as feminine, through their association with the Dyad. Furthermore, in a three-dimensional universe, it takes no less than four discrete steps to manifest and enwrap those three dimensions, hence the ancient association of quadrilaterals of all sorts (e.g., square, rectangle, cube, rectangular prism) with solidity and foundation.

Interestingly, the Biblical Hebrew (BH) word Maym is written with the use of only one letter. Recall that BH is a consonantal language, and as such is written exclusively with consonants. It order to aid pronunciation, vowels markings are inserted, but they are not considered in the gematria of BH words. Maym, which both begins and end with /m/, is formed from those two consonants, with vowel markings inserted to assist in the pronunciation of the word. *Maym is the only BH letter name to be written with only one letter.*

Linguistically, Maym is formed by the letter for matter completely enveloping two vowel sounds: /a/ and /y/. /a/ represents Aleph, the first letter of the AHA, thereby symbolizing spirit, while /y/ alludes to Yud, the tenth letter of the AB, which through its association with the Monad (i.e., 10 → 1+ 0 = 1), further reinforces the symbolism of Aleph. Hence, in terms of sound symbolism, we might interpret the BH word Maym as *"spirit ensconced in matter".*

In his deeply insightful text *The Wisdom in the Hebrew Alphabet*, Rabbi Munk (1983) asserts that the open and closed Mayms which respectively begin and end the letter name represent the revealed and concealed natures of God. The open Maym which begins the letter name represents the open, manifest, visible Glory of God, while the closed Maym which ends the letter name represents the impenetrable, recondite, unknowable mysteries of the Lord.

Munk (1983) further reveals that this dual nature of God is referenced in the story of Creation. The BH word Maym means "water". When God divides the waters above the firmament from the waters below the firmament, He is also figuratively both revealing and concealing His Will for humankind. The waters below the firmament are knowable, visible, and intelligible, while the waters above the firmament are unknowable, invisible, and unintelligible. According to Rabbi Munk (1983), the same symbolism is conveyed through the juxtaposition of the characters of

Moses, the revealer of God's Will in the Torah, and the Messiah, who represents the unknown aspects of God's Will.

In many situations, we are faced with both known and unknown variables. Wisdom is the ability to discern the difference between that which can be known, and that which either is unnecessary or not presently possible to know. As evinced by our daily existence, it is not necessary to know everything in order to survive. Indeed, one of the great joys of life is the fertile process of discovery, which would be entirely obliterated should even a single one of us possess omniscience! Perhaps it is instead a part of God's Greater Will that we continue to learn and grow, but never completely come to know. While we might quest eternally for greater understanding, to ultimately achieve such an end is to leave ourselves without a further destination. Perhaps God, in Infinite Wisdom, always reserves a little extra for us to seek and discover.

Nun: The Gift of New Life

The fourteenth letter of the Ancient Hebrew Alefbayt (AHA) is Nun. Phonetically speaking, the most unique and noticeable characteristic of the letter Nun is its articulatory height. /n/ is classified according to modern Linguistics as a "voiced alveolar nasal stop", indicating that while the vocal folds vibrate, air is shunted from the oral cavity into the nasal cavity (Burton, Dechaine, & Vatikiotis-Bateson, 2012, p. 44). As Kaplan (1997) expounds, the ancient Kabbalists instead classified Nun as a lingual, in that the sound is formed by pressing the tongue against the roof of the mouth, in such a way as to block the progression of air through the oral cavity, and instead to redirect it upwards into the nasal cavity. Hence, while the two descriptions are different in the details, they largely concur on the major aspects of articulation.

If you close your eyes, and hum the sound /n/, you will feel the primary resonance of the letter high up in the face, even as high as the cheekbones (though of course the actual area of resonance is the nasal cavity). *Indeed, of all the letters in the AHA, Nun is pronounced at the highest point in the vocal tract*, indicating its prominence as a letter of hope, inspiration, and faith.

Rabbi Munk (1983, p. 156) shares that in Aramaic, the word Nun means "fish", which is a source of nourishment and sustenance to the body. In the same way, faith in God nourishes, protects, and sustains the spiritual aspects of human beings. Munk (1983) also points out that fish are associated with productiveness and rebirth, in much the same way that we contemporarily think of rabbits. Fish lay thousands of eggs at a time and reproduce rapidly. As will be further supported by evidence from the gematria of Nun, there is a strong theme of re-birth and re-generation which runs through its interpretation.

The numeric essence of Nun distills down to an association with the Pentad, whether we consider that its gematria is 50 (5 + 0 = 5), or if we consider that it is the 14th letter (1 + 4 = 5). Recall that through its association with the Pentad, which houses never-ending variations on the numeric ratio phi (i.e., the Golden Ratio), the fifth serial letter, He, is strongly associated with the archetype of life. However, whereas the number 5 is a single digit and therefore associated with life itself, through Nun we arrive at the second iteration of the number 5. Hence, rather than a simple issuance of life, Nun represents a state of renewal or rebirth.

Whereas the Pentad and the corresponding letter He are closely associated with life, the letter Nun is instead associated with *new life*, or re-birth. Another way of looking at this is that it represents not so much a physical birth as a metaphoric birth. For example, this is the re-birth that occurs when a person is renewed in their faith and zeal, whatever their religion might be. They are already physically alive; however, they are in a sense *reborn* through a new outlook, a new perspective, and a new perception of events. This rebirth can be a completely transformative experience in the minds and hearts of the person so awakened.

In addition to all of these considerations, a set of patterns has emerged through the research and reflection associated with preparing this article. If we are to follow the basic map of the AHA set out by the mother letters, and reemphasized by the first three letters, we can discern the following pattern:

Aleph is the first mother letter, and as a phone produced deep in the hidden recesses of the vocal tract represents spirit.

Maym is the second mother letter, and as a phone produced overtly at the front of the vocal tract represents matter.

Shin is the third mother letter, and as a phone produced intermediately between the front and back of the vocal tract represents that which connects spirit and matter, or mind.

This categorization is further supported by the first three serial letters of the AHA, namely Aleph, Bayt, and Gimel. *The first three serial letters of the AHA follow the exact same phonetic pattern as the three mother letters.* That is, Aleph is a guttural letter, Bayt is a labial letter, and Gimel as a palatal consonant is produced intermediately between them in the vocal tract.

If we further extend this pattern to the Ennead, which is essentially a trinity of trinities, we can establish a discernible map which will aid in our analysis and evaluation of the first nine letters of the AHA:

The numbers 1-3 represent the **Spiritual Triad** of the Ennead.

The numbers 4-6 represent the **Material Triad** of the Ennead.

The numbers 7-9 represent the **Mental Triad** of the Ennead.

Finally, we do appear to be within rights to expand this pattern one final time to the Heptad, as the total AHA comprises 22 letters, which in Brotherhood of Light tradition is composed of 3 groups of 7, with a final capstone uniting and completing the whole. If we apply this pattern, we arrive at the following reproducible motif, which can be superimposed upon the others previously mentioned, but also extends them further toward deeper analysis and interpretation:

The numbers 1-7 represent the **Spiritual Heptad**.

The numbers 8-14 represent the **Material Heptad**.

The numbers 15-21 represent the **Mental Heptad**.

The end goal of the process symbolized by the AHA is the realization of a state of perfect manifestation, or the introduction of a new form where none has previously existed. In order to do so, we must first consider the spiritual aspects of existence, followed by the simultaneous introduction of the physical and mental components of it which help to flesh it out.

We can complete our analysis of this framework for manifestation by appreciating that in the minds of the ancient mathematical philosophers, every ending formed a new beginning, and as such it is necessary to make allowance for this fact in our numeric system. Hence, the Tetrad (i.e., 4) is representative of the **product** or finished result of the building project that is represented by the progression from Monad through Dyad to Triad. The Decad reinforces the same symbolism as the Tetrad, being written 10, which can be taken to represent the Monad (1) raised to a new level of expression by the completion of one cycle (0). Finally, *the number 22 resonates with the identical ideal*, in that it is the third iteration of the Tetrad (i.e., 22 → 2 + 2 = 4; 400 = 4 + 0 + 0 = 4). This offers further confirmatory evidence that the number 22 represents the end result of the entire developmental process, as fully fleshed out through the same number of steps nested as an original trinity, a trinity of trinities, and a final trinity of heptads.

Hence, the structure of the AHA appears to depend upon a four-fold building process, as explained in detail in previous articles on the Tetrad and Decad. We can make sense of this fascinating structure through bringing back to mind a bedrock fact that is true anywhere, at any time in the universe: *it requires no less than 4 discrete steps to move from a state of conception to a three-dimensional figure* (Taylor, 1816). Geometrically, this is represented as the movement from the dimensionless point (Monad), to the one-dimensional line (Dyad), to the two-dimensional plane (Triad), and finally to the three-dimensional shape (Tetrad). This line of reasoning is further confirmed by the fact that in our numbering system, 1 + 2 + 3 + 4 = 10, indicating that in the minds of the ancients, a complete cycle, represented by 10, was completed in *no more or less than 4 steps.* This is also the origin of the construction of the Great Pyramid of Giza, as well as the famed Tetrakys of Pythagoras, all of which communicate the same symbolism, albeit in slightly different ways (Guthrie, 1988).

In consideration of these nested patterns, it can also be established that 14 is the second iteration of the Heptad (7 x 2 = 14), and therefore also bears relationships to this most spiritual of numbers. The Heptad (7), as the sum of the Triad (3) and the Tetrad (4), represents the spiritual quintessence (3) made manifest in the material world (4). Similarly to its role in music, the Heptad represents the completion and perfection of the scale, which then rebounds and renews upon itself (Schneider, 1994). The Heptad, however, as being the final whole number in the Spiritual Heptad series, represents the final stage of *spiritual* development, while 14 represents instead the final step towards *material* development. It is the original spark initiated with the Monad completing its material assembly towards the end goal of perfect and complete manifestation.

SAMECH: TRANSFORMATION THROUGH TEMPTATION

The fifteenth letter of the Ancient Hebrew Alefbayt (AHA) is Samech. Munk (1983) shares that the shape of Samech renders it a symbol of God's protection and shelter, for the letter is completely enclosed, in the same way that God encloses and safeguards us. Samech also begins the Bibical Hebrew (BH) word for secret, sod, and the BH word sefirah, hence its use as a symbol of that which is hidden or mysterious.

Linguistically, Kaplan (1997) remarks that the ancient Kabbalists classified Samech as a dental, indicating that it is formed near the teeth. As a dental, Samech most closely aligns with the mother letter Shin, which is representative of the mind. Recall that Aleph, as a sound produced deep in the throat hidden from view represents spirit, while Maym, produced overtly at the lips represents matter.

Samech has an identical pronunciation to Shin, further supporting a link between the two letters. Based on these associations, we can conclude that the primary interpretive level of Samech pertains to the mind. However, the second letter of the word Samech, Maym, pertains to matter. Finally, the third and final sound of the word Samech, Chayt, is most closely associated with rebirth and regeneration. Hence, we can render at least one interpretation of the AHA letter Samech as: *transformation of the mind through the body*. This also aligns closely with one of the most interesting interpretive points of the letter Samech, the Kabbalistic meaning of Satan.

In Christian belief, Satan is anthropomorphized as the archenemy of God, and is to be feared and guarded against. Perhaps this is one interpretation of the meaning of Satan, but the Kabbalistic explanation is more internal and personal than that. As Yardeni (2015) insightfully explains, in Kabbalistic thought, Satan is typically translated as "adversary" or "disturber". The battle with the Satan is less external and more internal. Satan is seen as the selfish desire that we must all overcome on our way to greater expansiveness of mind. In this sense, Satan is never really born and never really dies, but is always there, lurking in the darkest corners of our minds, examining all instances for the benefit to self. One might equate Jung's account of the Shadow with a similar theme; in order to rise to higher and higher levels of spiritual insight and ability, the selfish urge must be transmuted and converted into the desire to do unto others as we would have done unto ourselves (Stevens, 2010). By considering not only what is beneficial to us, but that which operates in the interest of the Greatest Good for all, we have vanquished the evil foe, at least in that moment.

Kabbalistically, then, Satan represents the point of temptation that exists within all of us at all times. There is never a moment when we can completely turn our backs on the possibility of selfishness, just as there is never a time when we should stop seeking to advance and grow spiritually. Paradoxically, it is in *not* pursuing spiritual growth that we grow the most. That is, if we are seeking spiritual growth for our own gratification, to placate and appease the ego of attainment, we will only succeed in stepping further and further away from our goal. Rather, it is only through truly selfless, charitable acts, whether formal or informal, that we transform our souls, vanquishing the fiendish foe, and entering upon the light of eternal glory.

AYIN: BELIEVING IS SEEING

The sixteenth letter of the Ancient Hebrew Alefbayt (AHA) is the letter Ayin. Ayin is one of only two silent letters in the entire AHA, the other being the mother letter, Aleph. Recall that Aleph, as the first letter of the AHA, represents the ineffable nature of God (Munk, 1983). The fact that Aleph is a silent letter, and can therefore never truly be pronounced, stands as an eternal reminder that the nature of God can never fully be comprehended. Likewise, Ayin has to do with ideas and concepts that relate to the inner rather than the outer plane. It is closely tied to spirituality, and expresses itself clearly in our mentality.

Rabbi Munk (1983, p.171) reveals that the word Ayin means "eye" in Biblical Hebrew (BH), and the connection to our most dominant sense is apt. As opposed to addressing sight on the outer plane, however, the letter Ayin is an admonition to practice what we might term *right sight* on the inner plane (i.e., perception). There is an old saying that *perception is reality*, and while there are of course limitations to this statement, it is still a valuable axiom. As sentient beings, we express some level of control over our environment, but we must also acknowledge that there are many aspects of our lives over which we exert little power. If a natural disaster blows into town, we are often at the mercy of the elements in terms of our survival and welfare. If the object of our affections decides that she no longer wishes to be so, after all that is her right, and we are left to understand and comprehend the new situation in which we find ourselves.

Still, while there are situations in which we exert little control over our external environment, *we always retain the ability to decide how to respond to any event that impacts us.* That is, we retain the right to develop our own *perception* of the matter.

Psychologists acutely remind us time and again that it is the perception of the event, and not necessarily the event itself, which determines the impact on the psyche. Thus, two people experiencing the exact same event can have totally different psychological responses, because while seeing is believing, in many ways *believing is also seeing.*

In the moment we are afflicted by a tragedy, a loss, or some other untoward event, we have a critical, though often subconscious, decision to make. While we cannot change the outward circumstances of our lives, we always retain the ability to react to that tragedy in a positive, constructive way. While it may take months or years to seek and discover that point of equilibrium, we all have it within ourselves to ultimately come to a point of acceptance and in some cases even an appreciation of any positive outcomes which may have been precipitated by even the most challenging events of our lives.

The moral of Ayin does not address our physical sight, but rather deals with the all-important aspect of our inner sight, our perception of the events which befall us. Phonosemantically, this is also ingeniously concealed within the construction of the word itself. The word Ayin is composed of the letters Ayin (guttural), Yod, (palatal), and Nun, (lingual). Recall that the theory of phonosemantics states that the sounds which comprise words are not completely arbitrary, but rather that the sounds themselves communicate important aspects of meaning. The impacts of the sounds of the letters we use to construct language are often associated with and even constructive of the meaning of the word itself. This also appears to hold true in the case of Ayin.

The letter Ayin is a guttural, pronounced deep in the throat. It has been previously established that as sounds produced in the back of the throat are invisible and hidden from view, they represent well the concept of spirit. The second letter of the word Ayin, Yod, is a palatal, which allows the sound to advance further forward into the vocal tract, though it still retains a back position. The final letter of the word Ayin, Nun, is a lingual, pronounced by raising the tongue to the roof of the mouth and shunting the airstream up into the nasal cavity. *Importantly, notice that while the sound originates in the back of the throat, it never makes it to the front of the vocal tract (i.e., the lips), which is associated with matter.* Hence, even in the construction of the word itself, Ayin gives a clear picture of its inner nature. While it is represented by the eye, it is not concerned with the physical sense of vision so much as with the inner phenomenon of perception.

Finally, while we are free to interpret and respond to events however we see fit, perhaps it is wise to recall one final aspect of the sound symbolism of the word Ayin. The letter Nun, as the letter which is pronounced at the highest point of the vocal tract, represents those highest hopes, aspirations, and dreams that we possess. As such, Nun represents our sense of optimism and faith in our Creator, and the world which that Creator has produced that we might experience life, love, and light. We certainly would not act in error to pass all of our experiences through the filter of hope as we seek to interpret and understand our world.

THE POWER OF PAY

The seventeenth letter of the Ancient Hebrew Alefbayt (AHA) is the letter Pay. Munk (1983, p. 180) informs us that Pay translates as "mouth", and so more than any other archetypal consonant has to do with the unique human capacity for speech. In *The Holy Bible*, God creates the universe itself through the act of speech: "And God said, Let there be light: and there was light." (Genesis 1:3, The King James Version). God, the ultimate Creator of all things, manifests creation through the process of speech. This procedure is repeated several times, but in each case, it is through formulating His ideas and desires as words that God brings the universe into being.

In Kabbalistic literature, the process of speech is much more than a simple utterance of sound. It is representative of the entire creative process, even as applied to the creative processes of God (Munk, 1983, p. 19). This explains why the letters of the AHA take on an incredible level of import and value. If God employs the power of speech to create the universe, thereby converting ideas into reality, then we also may do the same, though of course on a much humbler scale. The process of speaking, then, is a metaphor for the creative process itself.

God created the universe through combining and recombining the archetypes represented by the letters in sundry ways, and we model the same process when we use these letters to create words and phrases to describe and delimit our own thoughts and ideas. In this sense, the letters of the AHA possess within themselves the unfathomable power of the universal creative process. However, it is critical to understand that in the mind of the Kabbalist, it is not only the sounds of the letters that have power, but even more so the archetypal concepts that they represent. As has been exposed in this text, each letter of the AHA represents a core idea, or archetype. As an example, Aleph, the very first letter of the AHA, is produced deep in the throat, out of sight, in much the same way that God, the Creator of the universe, nevertheless remains distinct and separate from Creation. Aleph, then, among other symbolic values, represents the concept of spirit- that which animates the material world, but which itself remains invisible and unknowable. This series of articles seeks to elaborate on the archetypal values of the AHA letters, though it is a part of the richness and beauty of this system that those archetypes are not singular and unidimensional, but can be conceived of by different people as implying different things, thereby adding to the richness of interpretation and homiletic value.

Modern linguistics classifies the letter Pay as a "*voiceless bilabial stop*" (Burton, Dechaine, & Vatikiotis-Bateson, 2012, p. 42). In other words, it is produced by ever so briefly blocking the flow of air behind the lips, and then allowing it to burst out in a soft puff of air. In terms of its articulation, it is formed in exactly the same manner as Bayt, however, Bayt is voiced (i.e., the vocal cords vibrate when it is produced), while Pay is unvoiced (i.e., the vocal cords do not vibrate when it is produced). As Catford (1988) describes in detail, you may experiment with this in your own vocal tract by placing your thumb and forefinger on your voicebox and humming. The buzzing sensation you feel is the activation of the vocal cords, which linguistically is called *voicing*. If you alternate humming and not humming with your fingers in this position, and you will quickly understand the distinction between voiced and unvoiced consonants. Once you are familiar with the complementary sensations of voiced and unvoiced consonants, alternately hum or do not hum while pursing the lips to form /b/ or /p/, respectively. If you pay careful attention, you will notice that *the shape of the vocal tract does not change* between these two letters. The only distinction between them is whether the vocal folds are recruited (voiced /b/) or remain unrecruited (unvoiced /p/).

Through an analysis of the letter Pay, the veil is lifted as to why the ancient Hebrew Sages attributed such import to the AHA. The AHA stands in as a representation of the creative process itself, up to and including the Creative Process of God. Through it, or rather through the symbolic combination and recombination of the basic elements of Creation, God creates and sustains the entire universe (Munk, 1983, p. 19). When we also wish to create something, we use words and phrases to artic-ulate, describe, and delimit our ideas. Whether these words are made audible through speech or remain undisclosed as thoughts, nevertheless, we must first formulate ideas and words before we can even begin to work toward their realization. The creation of *anything*, therefore, is first based on the organization of our desires into distinct, discrete thoughts, which we can then hold in mind through the power of concentration, applying a constant and unflinching effort, until they are made manifest in our world. This, then, is the true power of Pay.

TZADE: SPIRITUAL COMPLETION

The eighteenth letter of the Ancient Hebrew Alefbayt (AHA) is the letter Tzade. Tzade has a definite and focused association with the concept of righteousness. According to Munk (1983, p. 190), God is known by many names, among them Tzadik, "the Righteous One". Those who model their behavior on God's Perfect Rectitude here on Earth are also known as Tzadik. Munk (1983) further emphasizes that the process of becoming a Tzadik is never-ending, for as a person becomes more and more aware of God's Wisdom, the yearnings of her soul come to more and more completely dominate the urges of her body. Finally, Munk (1983) beautifully reminds us that while the physical body can and will decay across the lifespan, those who live righteously will continue to expand their knowledge, wisdom, and utility in God's Kingdom even as their bodes decline.

Phonosemantically, yet again we find a compelling concordance between the intent of the letter Tzade and its point of articulation in the vocal tract. The first letter of the word Tzade is a composite sound made up of two distinct phones, /t/ and /z/. Tayt, the ninth letter of the Ancient Hebrew Alefbayt (AHA), is strongly associated with the Ennead, and therefore the concept of climax, completion, and realization. In the same way that the first inklings of an idea have their seeds in the Monad, which then progresses symbolically to its point of realization in the Ennead, so too is the completion of any process modeled by the progression from Monad to Ennead. Additionally, it is worth remembering that the ideal gestation of a human being is estimated at 9 months, an idea which could easily have played in the minds of the ancient Hebrew Sages when they conceived of the decimal numbering system itself. Finally, as a *trinity of trinities*, the Ennead (and by extension, Tayt) represents spiritual, physical, and mental completion.

The second phone of the composite sound /tz/ is /z/. As the seventh letter, Zayin is closely associated with the Heptad. Of all the numbers within the Decad, the Heptad (7) is most closely associated with the Monad (1), which symbolizes the perfection and unity of God (Schneider, 1994). Mathematically, there are several justifications for this association. Schneider (1994, p. 224) further reveals that the Heptad was anciently known as "virgin", as no other number in the Decad enters into it evenly (e.g., as 2 enters into 4, or as 3 enters into 6 and 9). It was also called "childless", as it cannot produce any number within the Decad through multiplication (as 2 produces 4, or as 3 produces 6 and 9). Furthermore, neither 1 nor 7 can be expressed as a product of any two whole numbers except for itself and 1 (i.e., they are prime). Finally, 7 is the only number between 1 and 10 that cannot enter evenly into 360, the number of degrees in a circle. *For this final reason, it is physically impossible to draw a perfect Heptagon, while it is possible to draw all other polygonal figures within the Decad.* The Ancients saw in these facts the symbolism of an entity that remains forever beyond the profane world of the here and now. They saw in it the light in the darkness; an eternal reminder of the pure, spiritual state which animates and perpetuates the physical world, but which can never be completely reproduced by it.

As the first phone of Tzade is a composite sounds made up of /t/ and /z/, we can, among many other possible homiletic interpretations, summarize it as representing a state of *spiritual completion*. Those who have developed and matured sufficiently as to recognize the interconnectedness of all things cannot help but act in ways that support the dignity and purpose not only of their own interests, but of the entire universe. They are ever guided towards behaving and acting in ways that foster the greater good and Divine Intent of the world. This is in essence a restatement of Zain's (1998, p. 89) Universal Moral Code, "A soul is completely moral when it is contributing its utmost to cosmic welfare." When a person constantly strives to put others before self, to take their fair share but no more, even in the face of temptation or opportunity, and when they are able to apply this ability consistently and even joyously, then we may begin to believe that they are truly modeling the Tzadik, "the Righteous One" (Munk, 1983, p. 190).

Quph: Life in Death

The nineteenth letter of the Ancient Hebrew Alefbayt (AHA) is Quph. Quph begins several Biblical Hebrew (BH) words, the analysis of which can help us to penetrate and expose its meaning. In his text *The Hebrew Alphabet*, Hoffman (1998, p. 75) informs us that Quph begins the word "kedushah" or *holiness*, and is therefore associated both with The Holy One, God, as well as those on earth who continually purify themselves so that they live more and more in line with God's purpose. It also begins the BH word "korban" or *sacrifice*, a meaning into which we will delve deeply in this article. Finally, it begins the word that encompasses all of our efforts in this series of articles, "kabbalah", meaning *to receive*. This word can be interpreted in at least a dual sense, in that the mystic teachings of the Jewish people known as Kabbalah are reputed to have been received from God Himself, as well as in the fact that each generation receives these secret teachings of wisdom from the one before it.

According to modern linguistic theory, the letter /k/ is classified as a *"voiceless velar stop"* (Burton, Dechaine, & Vatiki-otis-Bateson, 2012, p. 42). This means that it is pronounced by approximating the tongue to the velum, or soft palate, at the back of the roof of the mouth. Kaplan (1997) reports that the ancient Hebrew Sages defined the letter /k/ as a *palatal*, an assignment that more or less concurs with the modern classification. Based on its point of articulation in the middle of the mouth, we can posit that the letter Quph is associated with the mind, as opposed to spirit or matter. Recall that the former was most closely modeled by the mother letter, Aleph, in that it is pronounced deep in the throat, out of sight and invisible, in much the same way that spirit animates and enlivens all of existence, while always remaining distinct, separate, and untouched by the material level of existence. The latter, namely matter, is modeled most closely by the mother letter Maym, which is pronounced at the front of the mouth with the lips. Its pronunciation is overt, obvious, and manifest, in the same way that matter is the extrinsic expression of God's Creation. Those phones that are formed in the middle of the mouth, then, symbolize the bridge between spirit and matter, namely the mind.

In terms of its gematria, Quph has a double influence. As the third iteration of the Monad, (19 → 1 + 9 = 10 → 1 + 0 = 1), Quph bears an association with the Monad, the symbol of the perfection and completeness of God. Still, as it is the *third* iteration, it therefore connects to perfection of the mind. Recall that Quph begins such BH words as "kedushah", *holiness*, and "korban", *sacrifice* (Hoffman, 1998, p. 75). A disciple here on earth becomes most like God, and most fit to be called holy, when she has sacrificed the lower impulses and desires of the flesh on the altar of her heart, such that her thoughts and feelings becomes clean, pure, and unblemished in her efforts to serve God. In a sense, it is through the death of the lower self that the higher self is born into being, ready and willing to serve the Lord as fully and deeply as possible.

The design and construction of the word Quph also reveals the meaning and intent of this AHA letter. In BH, the word Quph is composed of three letters: Q, U, Ph. Munk (1983) relates that the first letter, Quph, is a composite letter made up of a Waw (6) and a Raysh (20). Hence, in terms of its gematria, Quph has a value of 26, which is identical to the Divine Name, Yahweh. This bespeaks a strong association with The Holy One, or God. The second letter of the letter name Quph, Waw, means "hook"- in other words, that which is attached to or connects to another (Benner, 2019). Interestingly, in terms of its articulation, the sound /w/ is pronounced by rounding the lips into a shape that is also reminiscent of the perfection and completion of the circle, symbol of the Monad, and therefore God. Here again, we see a hint at the holiness associated with this letter. Finally, the letter /p/ (which when aspirated in BH is pronounced as /ph/), is most strongly associated with the unique human capacity for speech. Recall that in Kabbalistic tradition, God is said to have created the entire universe through the capacity of speech (Munk, p. 19). Viewed in this manner, the letters of the AHA take on extraordinary spiritual significance as the building blocks of Creation itself. Recall that in addition to representing the sounds that give shape and substance to our thought and words, the letters of the AHA stand in as archetypes that represent fundamental concepts employed in the construction of the universe. In the same way that God uses those archetypes to form the substance of Creation, we model that process by employing those same archetypes to create our best lives.

Synthesizing the various meanings of these word parts, we can derive the symbolism of Quph as *holiness in thought, word, and deed*. Indeed, those who selflessly sacrifice themselves for the greater good and welfare of the whole are often the most revered among us, as is well evinced by the lives of inspirational figures such as Jesus Christ, Dr. Martin Luther King, Jr., and Mahatma Gandhi. Whether that sacrifice is literal or figurative, it is through the immolation of the lower self that the higher self rises like the morning sun, come back to renew the world after its sacrifice and death the previous evening.

Raysh: Mercurial Magic

The twentieth letter of the Ancient Hebrew Alefbayt (AHA) is Raysh. Hoffman (1998, p. 77) informs us that Raysh begins several Biblical Hebrew (BH) words, such as "*ruach*", which means *wind, breath, or spirit*, as in the phrase "Ruach Ha-Kadosh", or "*The Holy Spirit*". It also begins the BH words "*rafooah*", *healing*, as well as "*rofah*", *healer* (Hoffman, 1998, p. 78). Finally, it begins the very well-known Hebrew word, *rabbi*, which means *master*, but has taken on the more colloquial and accessible meaning of *teacher*. As disparate as all of these terms may appear at first blush, they actually unite under a single archetype that is well known and understood by students of esotericism: the symbolism and conceptualization of the planet Mercury.

Based on the original correspondences established at the beginning of this series of articles, the heavenly influence with which Raysh is most closely associated is the planet, Mercury. Mercury is the swiftest of the planets, completing its revolution of the sun in a mere 88 days. It demonstrates extremes of temperature, varying at its coldest and hottest points from -275 °F to 840 °F respectively, a difference of over 1,100°F (Choi, 2017)! These characteristics (and many more) worked their way into the anthropomorphic representation of the planet as the god, Mercury. Mercury is the swift-footed messenger god depicted with winged sandals that carry him on the wind. Perhaps through Mercury's association with the intellect and mind, he is also the god of medicine and healing. Finally, Mercury is known as the most changeable of the gods, which also shows through in an analysis of the planet's physical characteristics.

As explained by Hickey (1992, p. 30), the symbols of the planets are formed through the unification of three fundamental shapes: the circle, representing spirit, the crescent, representing the mind, and the cross, representing the body. The astronomical symbol of Mercury is depicted as follows:

This ancient symbol clearly shows that in the case of Mercury, the intellect dominates the spirit and body. While all three elements are depicted, there is a distinct imbalance between them, with mind overriding the rightful place of spirit. Hence, those governed by the planet Mercury are said to be intellectual, probing, scientific, and penetrating, but must guard against the pitfall of missing the bigger picture of the role of investigation and study in the overall scheme of nature. Those with Mercury prominent may analyze very well, but must take special care to *synthesize* in order to properly place the intellectual process into its broader, spiritual context.

Linguistically, the letter Raysh coincides with the energy and character ☿ of Mercury. In at least one of its forms, it is produced through a rapid alteration of the tongue, creating the familiar trilled /r/ of romance languages such as Spanish or Italian. Linguistically, the English /r/ is classified as a *"palato-alveolar approximant"*, meaning that it is produced through narrowing but not completely blocking the air flow between the tongue and the roof of the mouth just behind the teeth at the alveolar ridge (Burton, Dechaine, & Vatikiotis-Bateson, 2012, p. 45). Very interestingly, while Raysh is often pronounced in modern

Hebrew as a guttural deep in the throat, the ancient Kabbalists classified it as a *dental*, indicating a much more forward placement than is contemporarily employed (Kaplan, 1997). While it would be interesting to explore how the pronunciation of /r/ has changed over time in Hebrew, such a study moves beyond the scope of the current investigation. As these articles are most concerned with the relationship between sound and meaning in Biblical Hebrew, this is the avenue that will be further examined.

Continuing, then, with an analysis of the linguistic properties of Raysh, the letter demonstrates a dual nature that aligns well with the energy and concepts associated with Mercury. While Raysh begins many words that are associated with enlightenment, learning, and light, it also begins words such as "*rasha*", *wickedness* (Munk, 1983, p. 199). The same author elaborates that for the first time in the exploration of the AHA, a letter is denoted as having not only a positive message which expounds upon the existence and nature of God, but a negative manifestation which explores what happens to the person who steps away from God. This dual nature is fitting of a letter most closely associated with the changeable, malleable, mercurial nature of the closest planet to the sun.

Munk's (1983) message is ultimately positive, however, for even in hardship and suffering, God does not leave the sinner forsaken and forlorn, but rather celebrates her return. Munk shares this heart-warming, inspiring proclamation of God: "My children, make Me [just] a single opening of repentance the size of a needle point, and I will provide you with entrances through which wagons and carriages can pass" (Munk, 1983, p. 202). Truly, a God who can love and embrace the fallen so must be One who loves and directs the lives not only of the saints, but ultimately of sinners as well.

SHIN: HARMONY & BALANCE

Shin is the twenty-first serial letter and the third mother letter of the Ancient Hebrew Alefbayt (AHA). Whereas Aleph represents spirit and Maym represents matter, Shin represents the bridge between them, the state of harmony and balance which presides over all Creation, and which is expressed metaphorically as the mind.

As explained in the earlier article on *Aleph*, in Biblical Hebrew (BH) the first serial and mother letter was classified by the ancient linguists as a guttural consonant (Kaplan, 1997). It is formed *invisibly*, deep in the throat. Metaphorically, it corresponds well to spirit, which also is found in deep, invisible realms, providing an initiation point for all of Creation, but requiring further modification and manipulation in order to give rise to the incredible multiplicity of the Cosmos.

Maym, the second mother letter of the AHA, is conversely classified by ancient Hebrew linguists as a labial consonant, indicating that in order to pronounce it, it is necessary to bring the lips together, thus completely closing the mouth (Kaplan, 1997). In complete contradistinction to the guttural region of the vocal tract, the lips are entirely *visible*, and represent the most superficial portion of the vocal apparatus. Hence, figuratively, Maym represents that which is material, overt, and visible- in other words, matter.

The third and final mother letter, Shin, is pronounced at a point intermediate in the vocal tract, being classified by the ancient Hebrew linguists as a dental, indicating that it is formed primarily with the teeth (Kaplan, 1997). In order to phonate /sh/, a tunnel of sorts is created in the mouth which causes the air to strike the back of the teeth, resulting in the turbulent sound, /

sh/. *Hence, Shin is phonically a sound which is produced at a point of harmony between the extremes of Aleph and Maym.* Figuratively, it represents a point of compromise and communication between the invisible world of spirit and the visible world of matter: the mind.

In terms of gematria, the letter Shin is clearly associated with the Triad, also an ancient and abiding symbol of harmony. It is the 21st letter of the AHA (21 → 2+1=3), and is assigned a numerological value of 300 (300 → 3+0+0=3). Interestingly, the word Shin itself means "tooth", which may at least in one sense indicate its linguistic point of articulation.

The form of the letter Shin is, among other interpretations, emblematic of a deep and powerful paradigm in religious thought: the unity manifest as a trinity (Munk, 1983, p. 208). The letter is formed by three distinct upward strokes, all united into a single letter by a horizontal stroke at their base. Thus, the letter represents well the concept of a single, unperturbed, perfect unity, which manifests according to three distinct emanations in order to give rise to the world: spirit, body, and mind.

Taw: And the Last Shall be First

The twenty-second and final letter of the Ancient Hebrew Alefbayt (AHA) is Taw. Kabbalists classify the letter Taw as a lingual consonant, hinting at its deeper linguistic value (Kaplan, 1997). The same author explicates that linguals are one of five classes of consonants in the AHA. In order from most covert to most overt, the five classes are: *gutturals, palatals, linguals, dentals, and labials.* As now seems a sure and proper conclusion, *there does appear to be an intentional link between sound and symbolism in the design and construction of the AHA.* While the exact nature and extent of this phonosemantic link is yet to be determined, ample evidence has been offered through this series of articles to presuppose a connection, unless significant evidence to the contrary is presented.

As an example of the phonosemantic links discovered in the AHA, consider that consonants produced deep in the vocal tract, invisible and unseen, have been demonstrated to correspond to the unseen elements of the universe, namely the *spiritual* aspects of creation. Conversely, those speech sounds produced most superficially at the lips (i.e., labials) correspond in many cases to the most manifest aspects of nature, namely *material* objects and phenomena. Existing at an interface between them, lingual consonants provide an apt representation for the *mental* aspects of creation, operating as the intermediary between the spiritual and material elements of the universe.

Fittingly, we find in the name of the final letter of the AHA, Taw, an exact representation of this triune nature of the universe. The first letter, /t/, is a *lingual*, pronounced in the center of the vocal tract, and therefore corresponding to the *mental* plane. The vowel, /a/, is the very first letter of the AHA, Aleph. It is a *guttural* consonant, produced deep in the throat, and therefore represents the primacy of the *spiritual* aspects of creation. Finally, /w/ is a *labial*, pronounced at the lips, thereby completing the symbolism of Taw as also representing the *material* aspects of creation. Hence, in the seemingly unremarkable AHA letter *Taw*, what is most likely a deliberately constructed symbol of the triune nature of the universe is discovered, along with a concomitant representation of the spiritual, mental, and material aspects of existence.

According to Kaplan (1997, p. 8), the word *Taw* means "cross", and this symbolism is also apropos, as the cross has been used since time immemorial to represent a state of balance and order as regards the three main elements of Creation. The astronomical symbol of the earth, $\oplus$, which is a cross inside a circle, demonstrates the three aspects of creation in perfect symmetry and balance. The circle represents the infinite, unchanging, immutable quality of *spirit*. The horizontal line represents the mundane element of *matter*, while the vertical line represents the inward, aspiring aspects of character and *mentality*. In the geometric relationship represented by the cross, these three composite elements of the universe are arranged in perfect harmony. As this is the astronomical symbol of our planet, homiletically, we might interpret this to mean that at its heart, the purpose of our planet, Earth, is to help God's children discover a similar state of spiritual, physical, and mental harmony. Of course, this is much easier said than done, and so represents a very worthy target regardless of one's present point of development along the path to spiritual attainment. Indeed, it is not unfair to say that the person who proclaims that they are "enlightened" is by that very same statement impugned, in that enlightenment is more effectively conceptualized as a *journey* rather than a *destination*.

If we are to take our cues from Nature, She remains in constant pursuit of greater development and growth. Being a part of nature, then, we also must fall quite in line with this same *modus operandi*.

In a manner similar to the analysis of the letters that constitute the word Taw, there is another Biblical Hebrew (BH) word equally worthy of consideration. In *The Wisdom in the Hebrew Alphabet*, Rabbi Munk (1983, p. 214) dedicates nearly his entire chapter on the letter Taw to the concept of *"Emet"*, or *Truth*. Having analyzed all the letters of the AHA through a phonosemantic lens, we are now in a position to more deeply understand what appears to be the deliberate construction of the BH word *"Emet"*. The first letter, Aleph, is the first letter of the AHA, a *guttural* produced deep in the throat, and as such representative of *spirit*. The second letter, Maym, is a *labial* consonant, articulated at the lips, and thus indicative of *matter*. Finally, the letter Taw, as amply discussed here, is the final letter of the AHA and a *lingual* consonant produced in the middle of the vocal tract, and thus symbolic of the *mental* plane. Taken together, the letters yet again represent a state of symmetry, order, and balance between the three fundamental elements of Creation. Hence, the construction of the BH word for *Truth*, *Emet*, stands in as a symbol itself of truth, in that it represents a unified, absolutely symmetric relationship between the three prime elements of the universe: spirit, matter, and mind. Further supporting this analysis is the fact that the three letters that comprise the BH word *Emet* are the first, middle, and last letters of the AHA. Hence, there is not only a symmetry and order regarding the basic elements of the universe, but also a positional symmetry which accounts for *all* of the letters of the AHA, as well as the archetypes they represent, within a neat and tidy package of three letters. Now that is a word worthy of representing the lofty concept of *Truth*!

In the minds of the ancient Kabbalists, every ending brought with it a state and sense of completion, but also planted the seed of a new beginning. A mature plant has not fulfilled its mission until it has gone to seed, laying out the conditions for the next generation to rise where it ultimately must fall. Similarly, the letter Taw is the capstone that completes and unites the AHA. And yet, it also functions as the cornerstone of a new and even grander edifice, built upon the strength and structure of the original foundation. For with the twenty-two letters of the AHA, human beings construct a nearly infinite number of words that allow us to describe and communicate our unique experiences to each other. Fittingly, while we all exist within the same Creation, our indulplicable vantage points guarantee a novel experience for all. Through the gift of language, we share our stories as if around campfires, enlightening and engaging each other in the common celebration of life.

Furthermore, as the letters of the AHA stand in as symbols of the very essences of life itself- ancient archetypes that are as relevant today as there were when they were first described- the study of the AHA is concomitantly an investigation of the design and creation of the universe itself, replete with all the attendant mystery, fervor, and wonder such an enterprise warrants. It is a journey that never ends, and always promises greater discoveries around every corner.

THE SACRED HEBREW ALPHABET: SUMMARY & SYNTHESIS

The first article of this series on the Ancient Hebrew Alefbayt (AHA) was written for the Fall 2013 Quarterly of *The Brotherhood of Light*. Hence, this series of articles on the letters alone has traversed approximately six years of exploration, reflection, and consideration. If the articles on the Sacred Numbers as Archetypes are also included, this complete project has spanned a period of *nearly nine years*. The symbolism is apt; whether considering the archetype of the Ennead or the ninth letter of the AHA, Tayt, both have themes of climax and completion. This article, then, seeks to summarize and synthesize the information explored and discovered throughout this spiritual sojourn.

The second introductory article of the series on the AHA letters provided a large chart, primarily derived from Kaplan's (1997) *Sefer Yetzirah (p. 22, 178, & 198)*, a text well established as authoritative and insightful within the Kabbalistic tradition, with additional insights provided by the author. This graphic summarized key information and critical assumptions (e.g., astrological correspondences) made at the onset of this project. For convenience and to encourage reflection and juxtaposition, I am reprinting it below, *with a row added below each entry which includes* **Keywords and Essential Descriptions**, based on both General (G) and Phonosemantic (P) symbolisms uncovered through the process of researching and generating these articles.

Importantly, the reader will note that the AHA letters are *not* presented below in sequential order. While there are potential merits to such a presentation, it is the opinion of the author that the pattern presented below- specifically, of grouping the letters according to their status as Mother, Double, or Single Letters- is of greater value and import than the sequential presentation of the AHA letters would be. There are powerful, determinative patterns present in the former style of presentation that can easily be occluded by a simple sequential description of the AHA letters. However, there is also value in a sequential description. Hence, while presenting the AHA letters according to the former grouping, the interpretations below will at times call on both categories of organization.

Finally, it is the deep and enthusiastic hope of the author that this information will materially contribute to what is known and understood about these several archetypes, especially as relates to the apparent phonosemantic elements of the Ancient Hebrew Alefbayt. No doubt, further research is required in this vein. Hence, it is also the humble hope of the author that others will endeavor to drive forward the understanding and interpretation of this valuable occult resource, and to further explore the vast repository of wisdom represented by the complementary arche-types of number and letter.

Letter	Name	Meaning	Number (Serial/Gematria/As a set of three clusters- Mother/Double/Single letter)	Designation	Kabbalistic Phonetic Grouping	Astrological Correspondence (Short Version, Raavad)
א	Aleph	Ox	1/1/1-1	Mother	Guttural	Pluto

General Symbolism (GS) of Aleph: 1st Mother Letter and 1st sequential letter of AB; God; Spirit; Unity; Oneness; Chaos, that which is invisible

Phonosemantic Symbolism (PS) of Aleph: A guttural consonant produced at the 1st articulatory position (i.e., throat). Sound produced deep in the throat, invisibly. As such, symbol of spirit- that which motivates and underpins manifestation, but can never be perfectly represented by it.

Letter	Name	Meaning	Number	Designation	Kabbalistic	Astrological
מ/ם	Maym/Final Maym	Water	13/4/1-2	Mother	Labial	Neptune

GS of Maym: 2nd Mother Letter and 13th sequential letter of AHA; Nature; Matter; Duality; that which is visible

PS of Maym: A labial consonant produced at the 5th articulatory position (i.e., lips). As its articulation is obvious to the viewer, so also is it symbolic of that which is overt, visible, and material.

Letter	Name	Meaning	Number	Designation	Kabbalistic	Astrological
ש	Shin	Tooth	21/300/1-3	Mother	Dental	Uranus

GS of Shin: 3rd Mother Letter and 21st sequential letter of AHA; Mind; Mentality; Astral Plane; Multiplicity; Harmony and Balance; Unity manifest as a Trinity

PS of Shin: A dental consonant produced intermediately at the 4th articulatory position (i.e., teeth). As such, representative of that which forms a link between spirit and matter, i.e., the mind.

Letter	Name	Meaning	Number	Designation	Kabbalistic	Astrological
ב	Bayt	House	2/2/2-1	Double	Labial	Saturn

GS of Bayt: 1st Double Letter and 2nd sequential letter of AHA; similarly to 2nd Mother Letter, Maym, relates to physicality and material world; universe as God's Home; body as soul's home; Duality; Principle of Opposites

PS of Bayt: A labial consonant produced at the 5th articulatory position (i.e., lips). Similarly to Maym, symbolic of that which is overt, visible, and material.

Letter	Name	Meaning	Number	Designation	Kabbalistic	Astrological
ג	Gimel	Camel	3/3/2-2	Double	Palatal	Jupiter

GS of Gimel: 2nd Double Letter and 3rd sequential letter of AHA; similarly to 3rd Mother Letter, Shin, relates to mind and astral plane; Principle of Harmony, Equilibrium, Balance

PS of Gimel: A palatal consonant produced at the 2nd articulatory position (i.e., palate). Represents a bridge between spirit and matter, or more properly between spirit and mind, owing to its articulatory position.

Letter	Name	Meaning	Number	Designation	Kabbalistic	Astrological
ד	Dalet	Door	4/4/2-3	Double	Lingual	Mars

GS of Dalet: 3rd Double Letter and 4th sequential letter of AHA; "Door" through which manifestation occurs; Tetrad as symbol of completion of four-fold process of creation; Tetrakys of Pythagoras

PS of Dalet: A lingual consonant produced at the 3rd (central) articulatory position. Symbolic of the completion of one process and the concomitant initiation of a new plane of action.

Letter	Name	Meaning	Number	Designation	Kabbalistic	Astrological
כ/ך	Kaph/Final Kaph	The hand bent	11/20/2-4	Double	Palatal	Sun

GS of Kaph: 4th Double Letter and 11th sequential letter of AHA; Movement from spirit to matter.

PS of Kaph: A palatal consonant produced at the 2nd articulatory position. Strong correlation between phonation and semantic value. Symbolic of movement from spirit to matter.

כ/ך	Pay/Final Pay	Mouth	17/80/2-5	Double	Labial	Venus

GS of Pay: 5th Double Letter and 17th sequential letter of AHA; Process of speech production as a metaphor for creative process; Letters of AHA as archetypes of building blocks of universe itself.

PS of Pay: A labial consonant produced at the 5th articulatory position. As God used letters (or more properly, archetypes represented by letters) to create universe and all within it, God gifts us with the ability to follow suit on a smaller scale by using language to formulate and communicate ideas.

ר	Raysh	Head	20/200/2-6	Double	Dental	Mercury

GS of Raysh: 6th Double Letter and 20th sequential letter of AHA; Closely tied to symbolism of Mercury, planet associated with it; As such, swiftly and rapidly produced phonetically; changeable in its production and manifestation; Intellect as dominating spirit and matter.

PS of Raysh: A dental consonant produced at the 4th articulatory position. At least in one variation, produced through rapid alteration of tongue (i.e., trill). Speed and changeability of Mercury evident information of phone.

ת	Taw	Cross	22/400/2-7	Double	Lingual	Moon

GS of Taw: 7th **(final)** Double Letter and 22nd **(final)** letter of AHA; Symbolic of completion, realization, process of creation brought to fruition; Associated with ancient symbol of the cross, itself formed through an ideal balance of spirit (circle), body (horizontal line), and mind (vertical line).

PS of Taw: A lingual consonant produced at the 3rd (central) articulatory position. A near-perfect phonetic representation of its semantic value (i.e., meaning). Three sounds that compose it (namely, /t/, /a/, and /w/) are lingual, guttural, and labial, respectively. Phonosemantically, symbolic of state of harmony and balance between three universal forces of mind, spirit, and matter. BH word "emet", or "truth", formed in a similar fashion, phonetically capturing its semantic intention.

ה	He	Window	5/5/3-1	Single	Guttural	Aries

GS of He: 1st Single Letter and 5th sequential letter of AHA; Essentially an audible breath, symbolic of life itself, and all of the complexity and grandeur this entails; Self-replication; Life from life, breath from breath; 4 elements under the proper and healthful dominion of mind, or if inverted, lower desires overshadowing reason; Associated with Aries, first sign of Zodiac and representative of new life; Golden Mean (i.e., *phi*) as ubiquitous form of adaptable symmetry in living things.

PS of He: A guttural consonant produced at the 1st articulatory position. Through its association with the mother letter Aleph (as a guttural consonant), symbolic of spirit, that which animates and orchestrates life.

ו	Waw	Hook	6/6/3-2	Single	Labial	Taurus

GS of Waw: 2nd Single Letter and 6th sequential letter of AHA; for clear and correct phonosemantic analysis, must be considered as *labial*, not dental as in modern pronunciation (i.e., Vav); Symbol of symmetry and physical perfection; 3 dimensions of space producing 6 directions; 1st perfect number (i.e., 1 + 2 + 3 = 6); also produced by multiplication of factors (i.e., 1 x 2 x 3 = 6); by corollary, also demonstrates arithmetic symmetry subtractively and divisionally.

PS of Waw: A labial consonant produced at the 5th articulatory position. Name of letter itself (i.e., Waw) is perfectly symmetric and balanced; First letter of AHA to demonstrate such an overt state of symmetry; Strong correlation between phonetic pronunciation and semantic value.

ז	Zayin	Weapon	7/7/3-3	Single	Dental	Gemini

GS of Zayin: 3rd Single Letter and 7th sequential letter of AHA; Through association with Heptad, symbolic of presence of the divine in the mundane, spirit as animating matter; Heptagon is *only* geometric shape within Decad that can never be drawn exactly, a reminder that physical can approach, but never fully capture, spiritual essence; Symbolic of very familiar form of harmony seen in seven-fold musical scale.

PS of Zayin: A dental consonant produced at the 4th articulatory position. Yod, symbolic of spirit, lies concealed within letter name; symbolic of spirit as residing in matter.

ח	Chayt	Fence	8/8/3-4	Single	Guttural	Cancer

GS of Chayt: 4th Single Letter and 8th sequential letter of AHA; Symbolic of death and re-birth; Octad as completion of one cycle and concomitant commencement of next; Begins BH word for "sin", which is representative of a metaphoric death, as it takes actor further from God; Also begins BH word for "life", reinforcing dual symbolism of death and rebirth.

PS of Chayt: A guttural consonant produced at the 1st articulatory position. /ch/ sound indicative of dissolution and chaos of death; /y/ represents spark of life that simultaneously ends and begins a new cycle (/t/).

ט	Tayt	Snake	9/9/3-5	Single	Lingual	Leo

GS of Tayt: 5th Single Letter and 9th sequential letter of AHA; through its association with the Ennead, symbolic of climax and completion of process that began with Monad; "Harmony of Harmonies"; "Trinity of Trinities"; Synthesis of 1st (Spiritual) Triad, 2nd (Physical) Triad, and 3rd (Mental) Triad represented by single digits up to and including the Ennead (9).

PS of Tayt: A lingual consonant produced at the 3rd articulatory position; articulatory position of Tayt itself demonstrates balance, as it is the *most central* of the articulatory positions; Tayt also literally acts as a "Harmony of Harmonies" phonosemantically, in that it is pronounced intermediate to Gimel (3rd sequential letter) and Waw (6th sequential letter), each of which concludes a Triad within the Decad.

'	Yod	Hand	10/10/3-6	Single	Palatal	Virgo

GS of Yod: 6th Single Letter and 10th sequential letter of AHA; as first double-digit number, symbolic of Multiplicity as Unity; "10" is perfect representation of this concept, as it is comprised of "1", a unity, and "0", an overt symbol of a completed cycle; symbolizes completion of one round of activity and simultaneous introduction of a new level of progression.

PS of Yod: A palatal consonant produced at the 2nd articulatory position; as such, symbolic of bridge between spiritual and mental planes; only AHA letter than hangs suspended above the line, indicating movement to a new, higher plane of action.

ל	Lamed	Ox-goad	12/30/3-7	Single	Lingual	Libra

GS of Lamed: 7th (central) Single Letter and 12th (central) sequential letter of AHA; due to its doubly centralized position and sheer physical size as written, towering over all other letters, symbolic of a state of centrality, balance, and harmony; same principle reinforced by its gematria (Lamed = 30; 3 + 0 = 3; 12 → 1 + 2 = 3). Further reinforced still through its association with Libra, the sign that is emblematic of balance.

PS of Lamed: A lingual consonant produced at the 3rd articulatory position; as such, an excellent representation of aforementioned archetypes (i.e., centrality, harmony, balance), as it is formed in most central of five articulatory positions.

נ/ן	Nun/Final Nun	Fish	14/50/3-8	Single	Lingual	Scorpio

GS of Nun: 8th Single Letter and 14th sequential letter of AHA; through analysis of its Gematria (50 → 5 + 0 = 5; 14 → 1 + 4 = 5) symbolic of second iteration of Pentad (5), thus *new life, re-birth*; as it is AHA letter pronounced at highest point in vocal tract, figuratively interpreted as optimism, hope, faith, and inspiration; further, if system of 22 AHA letters is considered as 3 sets of 7, a **Spiritual Heptad (1-7), Material Heptad (8-14), and Mental Heptad (15-21)** arise. The 22nd letter shares a common symbolism with 4 and 10, representing the capstone (i.e., realization or manifestation) of the process originated with the Monad, as well as a simultaneous movement to a new level of expression.

PS of Nun: A lingual consonant produced at the 3rd articulatory position. As a *nasal* consonant, airstream is shunted up into the nasal cavity and emitted through the nose (i.e., no air leaves mouth). For this reason, Nun is AHA letter pronounced at *highest point in vocal tract.* As such, figuratively interpreted as optimism, hope, faith, and inspiration.

ס	Samech	Prop	15/60/3-9	Single	Dental	Sagittarius

GS of Samech: 9th Single Letter and 15th sequential letter of AHA; symbol of transformation of mind through triumph over material temptations; relates to Kabbalistic concept of "Satan", which is viewed as an internal, self-serving force that must be overcome in order to grow and develop spiritually; The Great Foe can be vanquished on a moment-to-moment basis, but constant vigilance is necessary, as the desire to serve self runs deep, and might even be described as instinctual.

PS of Samech: A dental consonant produced at the 4th articulatory position. The first letter of Samech, /s/, is pronounced identically to Shin, indicating a link with the mind. The second letter of Samech, /m/, relates to the body, (i.e., matter). Finally, the third letter of Samech, /ch/, relates to transformation and rebirth. Synthesizing these concepts, a possible interpretation of this word is *transformation of the mind through triumph over temptation in the body*. Here again, there is a strong relationship between the phonetics (sound) and semantics (meaning) of the AHA letter, Samech.

ע	Ayin	Eye	16/70/3-10	Single	Guttural	Capricorn

GS of Ayin: 10th Single Letter and 16th sequential letter of the AHA; one of only two silent letters in the AHA, the other being Aleph. Silent letters are an admonition to ever recall that the ineffable nature of God can never be completely captured on the physical plane; the word "Ayin" means eye, but combining this with its inner plane relationship, it refers not to physical sight, but to inner sight, or perception; the Kabbalists sagely remind us that while we may not be able to control all the events of our lives, we can always control our responses to those our events. This gives perception an exalted status in our lives.

PS of Ayin: A guttural consonant produced at the 1st articulatory position. The word "Ayin" is composed of three letters: /a/, /y/, and /n/. The first letter, /a/, is a guttural produced deep in the throat, indicative of its inner, spiritual foundation. The second letter, /y/ is a palatal produced slightly more forward in the mouth. The third letter, /n/, is a lingual produced in the center of the oral cavity. Thus, we see in the construction of the word "Ayin" a process of unfolding from the spiritual to the mental plane of activity. Notice that none of the letters move more forward than the middle of the mouth, demonstrating that the symbolism of Ayin relates to the spiritual and mental planes, but not as directly to the physical plane.

צ/ץ	Tzade/Final Tzade	Fish-hook	18/90/3-11	Single	Dental	Aquarius

GS of Tzade: 11th Single Letter and 18th sequential letter of AHA; symbolic of spiritual completion and righteousness.

PS of Tzade: A dental consonant produced at the 4th articulatory position. The first letter of Tzade, /tz/, is a composite sound make up of two distinct phones, /t/ and /z/. /t/ relates to Tayt, the ninth sequential letter of the AHA, as well as Taw, the 22nd and final sequential letter of the AHA. As such, /t/ represents a state of climax, completion, and closure. The second phone, /z/ relates to the 7th sequential letter, Zayin. Through its association with the Heptad, this letter is closely associated with spirituality and godliness. Recall that the heptagon is the only regular polygon which cannot be exactly circumscribed within a circle, and as such reminds us that while spirit can be approximated by matter, it can never be fully exemplified. Taken together, /tz/ can be interpreted as *spiritual completion*, a clear hallmark of the Tzadik, or righteous one.

ק	Quph	Back of the head	19/100/3-12	Single	Palatal	Pisces

GS of Quph: 12th Single Letter and 19th sequential letter of the AHA; Begins such BH words as *kedushah* (holiness), *karban* (sacrifice), and *kabbalah* (to receive). Based on its gematria ($100 \rightarrow 1 + 0 + 0 = 1$; $19 \rightarrow 1 + 9 = 10 \rightarrow 1 + 0 = 1$), closely associated with the Monad, and therefore God, Spirit, and Unity. Based on phonosemantic analysis (see below), can be interpreted as *holiness in thought, word, and deed*.

PS of Quph: A palatal consonant produced at the 2nd articulatory position. The first letter of Quph, /k/ relates to holiness and the spiritual plane. The second letter of Quph, /w/, is a labial consonant that relates to the physical plane. Finally, the third letter of Quph, /ph/ relates to the unique capacity for human speech, the production of which stands in as a metaphor for all creative acts, including God's construction of the universe through the formation of discrete archetypes and, representatively, the words that we use to express them.

121

References & Recommended Readings

Benner, J. (2019). *The ancient hebrew alphabet: Vav*. Ancient hebrew research center. https://www.ancient-hebrew.org/ancient-alphabet/vav.htm

Bolinger, Dwight (1950), "Rime, Assonance and Morpheme Analysis", *Word*, 6: 2,117-136.

Burton, S., Dechaine, R., & Vatikiotis-Bateson, E. (2012). *Linguistics for Dummies*. Missisauga, Ontario, CA: Wiley.

Catford, J.C. (1988). *A Practical Introduction to Phonetics*. New York, NY: Oxford University Press.

Choi, C.Q. (2017). *Planet mercury: Facts about the planet closest to the sun*. Space. https://www.space.com/36-mercury-the-suns-closest-planetary-neighbor.html

Garrett, D. (2008). *Wa or Va?* A modern grammar for biblical hebrew: A resource for students of the hebrew bible. http://hebrewgrammar.sbts.edu/page2/page2.html

Guthrie, K.S. (Ed.). (1988). *The Pythagorean Sourcebook and Library*. Grand Rapids, MI: Phanes Press.

Hickey, I. (1992). Astrology: *A cosmic science*. Sebastopol, CA: CRCS Publications.

Hoffman, E. (1998). *The hebrew alphabet*. San Francisco, CA: Chronicle Books.

Iamblichus. (1988). *The Theology of Arithmetic*. (Robin Waterfield, Trans.). Grand Rapids, MI: Phanes Press.

Kaplan, Aryeh. (1997). *Sefer Yetzirah: The Book of Creation*. Boston, MA: Weiser Books.

Kirtchuk, Pablo. (2011). *Hebrew*. HAL. https://hal.archives-ouvertes.fr/hal-00561422/document

Magnus, M. (2000). *What's in a Word? Evidence for Phonosemantics*. Trondheim, Norway: University of Trondheim dissertation.

Munk, Michael. (1983). *The Wisdom in the Hebrew Alphabet.* New York, NY: Mesorah Publications.

Nicomachus of Gerasa. (2015). *Introduction to Arithmetic* (J. Muscat, Trans.). (Original work published ca. 60-120 CE). http:// staff.um.edu.mt/jmus1/Nicomachus.pdf

Plato. (n.d.) *Cratylus.* B. Jowett (trans.) Available from: Amazon.com (Kindle version).

Schneider, M. (1994). *A Beginner's Guide to Constructing the Universe.* New York, NY: HarperPerennial.

Stevens, A (2010). *Jung: A very short introduction.* Available from Amazon.com (Kindle version.

Taylor, Thomas (1816). *Theoretic arithmetic.* Universal Theosophy. https://universaltheosophy.com/pdf-library/1816_ Theoretic-Arithmetic.pdf

Yardeni, E. (2015). *Is satan real?* The Kabbalah Centre. https:// kabbalah.com/en/articles/is-satan-real/

Zain, C.C. (1998). *Organic Alchemy: The universal law of soul progression.* Los Angeles, CA: The Church of Light.

Zain, C.C. (1994). *Sacred Tarot: The Art of Card Reading and the Underlying Spiritual Science.* Los Angeles, CA: The Church of Light.

ABOUT THE AUTHOR

Scenza is the pseudonym of Peter Tourian, a secondary science educator living in the greater New York City metropolitan area. A graduate of Yale University and Rutgers University, Peter has been associated with The Brotherhood of Light for nearly twenty years. He currently holds the positions of Certified Teacher and Hermetician within the organization. Peter resides in New Jersey with his wife, children, and their Vizsla, Charley.